Marketing Your Local Business Online

*Key Strategies to Increasing Sales and Profit
Using the Internet*

Sherry Han
Daisy Huang

www.GetInternetExposure.com

Copyright Notice

Copyright © 2012 by Sherry Han & Daisy Huang. All Rights Reserved.

Reproduction or translation of any part of this work beyond that permitted by section 107 or 108 of the 1976 United States Copyright Act without permission of the copyright owner is unlawful. Requests for permission or further information should be addressed to the author.

Sherry Han
P.O. Box 219042
Houston, TX 77218
United States

http://www.GetInternetExposure.com

This publication is designed to provide accurate and authoritative information in regard to the subject matter covered. However, its contents are based solely on the authors' personal experience and research. There are no guarantees concerning the level of success you may experience. Each individual's success depends on his or her background, dedication, desire and motivation.

First Printing, 2012

ISBN-13: 978-1480129085

ISBN-10: 1480129089

Printed in the United States of America

About the Authors

Sherry Han has been self-employed right out of college and never looked back. She began her Internet marketing career in 2000, while still in high school. She started off by selling imported goods on eBay. Since then, she has co-founded several successful companies, including a brick & mortar toy store.

Daisy Huang has been a full-time Internet marketer since 2006. While she has dabbled in many fields, her primary areas of expertise include video marketing, display advertising, and online lead generation for local businesses. She also enjoys writing and marketing books for various different niches in her free time.

They understand the intrinsic difficulties local businesses face when trying to attract new customers in our increasingly web-centric world. Together, they founded a company with the goal of helping local businesses gain much needed exposure on the Internet. To learn more about them, visit:

GetInternetExposure.com

Table of Contents

1. Why Take Your Marketing Online? 1
2. Your Website *"Your Piece of the Internet"* 7
3. Mobile Website *"Exposure On-the-Go"* 33
4. Local Listings *"e-Business Directories"* 39
5. Social Media *"Keeping Up With the Times"* 49
6. Video SEO *"No Steven Spielbergs Allowed"* 57
7. Reputation Management *"BBB of the Web"* 79
8. Other Important Internet Marketing Concepts 91
    I. Pay-Per-Click Advertising 91
    II. Groupon, LivingSocial, etc. 97
    III. Email Marketing 103
    IV. Tracking Phone Numbers 108
    V. Outsourcing 114
9. Conclusion 119

1. Why Take Your Marketing Online?

Over time, the Internet has literally become a way of life. We are constantly connected to it via desktop computers, laptops, smartphones, tablets, and PDAs. Frankly speaking, many of us simply cannot live without the Internet nowadays.

In addition, people are now more "on-the-go" than ever before. Why bother looking at print ads or billboards when it's so easy for one to whip out their iPhone and search for nearby restaurants, no matter where they are?

The Internet has become the number one tool for consumers to find local businesses, and the number of people using it is increasing by the day. If your business cannot be found on the most preferred medium for local information in the world, you **will** lose business to your competitors who can be found; plain and simple.

This book will introduce you to various web-based methods you can use to not only reach new clients, but also connect with existing ones.

Latest Search Engine Trends

The following chart shows the growth in Google searches since January 2008, according to comScore:

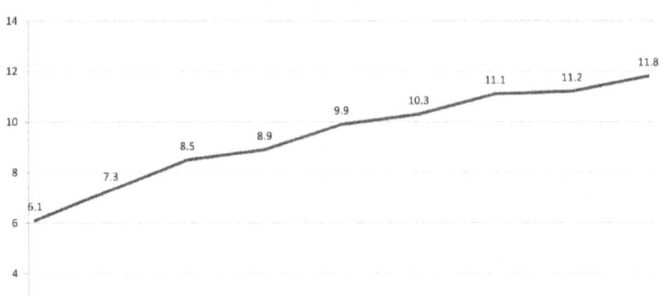

In only 4 years, the number of searches conducted on Google per month has nearly doubled. Google has officially stated that approximately 20% of all search queries are location specific. In January 2008, this number was 1.22 billion. In January 2012, it was a phenomenal 2.36 billion.

This trend has two important implications for you as a local business owner.

One, the number of local searches will continue to rise as time goes on. Not only are the older generations slowly adopting the Internet, the next generation is practically being raised in the digital world.

Two, print media such as magazine ads and the Yellow Pages will continue to decline in effectiveness until they eventually become obsolete. It's simply more convenient for a consumer to find local businesses online. Plus, on the Internet, the consumer can find a plethora of related information about a business that he or she may need. For instance, driving directions, product pictures, customer reviews, and so on.

Death of Print Media

Let's be honest here. When was the last time you actually picked up a Yellow Pages directory to find a service provider?

For me personally, this is what happened:

A few months ago, I noticed a Yellow Pages directory sitting next to my front door. I didn't pay much attention to it, and it sat there for two and a half months or so. Luckily it was wrapped in a plastic bag, because over time, it got rained on, stepped on, and bags of trash were piled up on top of it.

Then one day, I finally got sick of looking at the useless doormat. I picked up the dirty bag and shoved it into a trash bag, something I should have done a long time ago.

This is what's happening across the country, although maybe not exactly like how I described it. Indeed, for many people the directory goes straight into the trash the moment it's spotted.

Over a decade ago when I was still in high school, my mother would sometimes take me to visit her friends. I remember distinctively that many of them had the Yellow Pages directory sitting in the middle of the dining table, or on the kitchen counter. My parents used the directory pretty often themselves. Through the Yellow Pages they found their realtor, dentist, electrician, lawn mower, plumber... the list goes on.

Fast forward to the present, and literally nobody I know still owns a Yellow Pages directory, much less uses it. Even my parents and their peers have switched over to the Internet, and they're in their late 50's.

So as you can probably guess, you as a business owner have more incentives to advertise your business online as opposed to the Yellow Pages:

- Wider reach - search engines will showcase your business in front of more eyeballs than the Yellow Pages. The Yellow Pages directory is only distributed to households that still use landline phones, which nearly 25% don't. Moreover, as mentioned before, many of these directories are never used.
- More cost effective - a full page ad in the Yellow Pages can cost up to $10k per month! On the other hand, a listing for your business on Google is free to set up. You can pay to optimize and rank your listing, but the cost is not nearly as high for the same level of exposure.
- Personalization - you can only edit your Yellow Pages listing or advertisement prior to its publication, and any further changes to your business such as address or phone number will not be updated. In comparison, online advertising is easily customizable at any time, and you can personalize your business listings with photos, videos, news, special offers, and more.

To their credit, the Yellow Pages company did realize that they need to compete in the online medium. To do so, they set up a web version of their paper directory.

The problem is that they offer zero incentive for a consumer to use their web directory over Google. Why hop over to YP.com when you're already on Google, using Google search, Gmail, Google Docs, Google Calendar, Google Chat, and so on? Remember, Google is not just a search engine. Far from it! It's more like an all-in-one solution that includes most of the applications you'll ever need while online.

What about other print media, such as newspapers and magazines?

In many ways, television has already replaced these media outlets, and the Internet has all but obliterated them. When a newsworthy story happens, it's posted online virtually instantly (case in point - Twitter is the #1 site for getting updates on breaking news). Any article you read on a magazine is guaranteed to have been posted online quite some time ago.

Newspapers and magazines, save for the big names, have been struggling to pick up and retain subscribers in recent years. You can tell by the ridiculous "pennies-on-the-dollar" discounts they are constantly offering.

2. Your Website
"Your Piece of the Internet"

By now you've probably concluded that the Internet should be your number one priority when it comes to marketing your business. Not only in the near future, but very likely for many years to come.

The first step is to set up a website for your business. In all likelihood, you already have one. If not, there are hundreds of web design firms just around the corner you can contract the work to. Creating websites is not the focus of this book, and frankly the aesthetic design of your website isn't important, as long as it's presentable.

Remember, people are on your website to find information. They don't want to watch long flash videos (which iPhones and iPads can't even load), nor will they care that all your graphics are hand drawn. Your website should be simple and professional. Nothing more, nothing less.

Here are the main components of a successful local business website:

- NAP - **N**ame, **A**ddress, **P**hone. Add these three pieces of information to every page and keep them together. Google and other search engines look for this block of information to determine that you are, in fact, a local business.

- Basic company information - services you offer, service area, hours of operation, driving directions, prices, etc. Nowadays people want to find what they're looking for instantly. If potential customers have to call you to get answers, a lot of them won't even bother.

- A strong call to action - do you want prospective customers to call you? Fill out a form to request a quote? Sign up for your monthly newsletter? No matter what it is that you want, be sure to communicate it clearly near the top of your homepage. A clearly conveyed call to action steers viewers in the right direction. Without one, your conversion rate will surely drop.

- Industry specific information - for example, if you're an AC contractor, write articles or create videos about topics like properly maintaining an AC unit, troubleshooting common problems, choosing a new AC unit, and so on. Not only will you be seen as an authority on the topic, you're helping prospective customers out. In turn, they're more likely to return the favor by hiring you.

- Ample ways for (prospective) customers to contact you - I suggest having an entire "Contact Us" page set up on your business website. The page should include a form they can fill out to send an email to you, as well as your NAP.

- Customer reviews - people love social proof. The more positive customer reviews you can provide, the better. Syndicate reviews from your Google local listing, Yelp listing, etc. Also, whenever possible, provide video testimonials. It only takes a few minutes to record a testimonial from a happy client after you do business.
- Ways to keep in touch with (prospective) customers - your website needs links to your Facebook fan page, Twitter account, LinkedIn, etc. You should also keep a mailing list. Place the signup form somewhere on the front page where it's easy to find, and offer an incentive for signing up. For example, if you're an AC contractor, offer a discount on services or an AC maintenance guide.

Once your website has all of the above, it will help you achieve many important goals:

- Brand your business
- Establish your credibility as an industry expert
- Educate your (prospective) customers about your industry
- Help your (prospective) customers solve problems
- Give your (prospective) customers many ways to reach you
- Capture leads and subsequently generate sales

Moreover, Google loves informative websites with the components mentioned above, and such sites have a better chance at ranking highly in the search engines. More on this later.

One important thing to keep in mind is that you should not try to cram all this information onto your homepage. Each page should have a specific topic or purpose. Going back to our AC contractor example, the services you offer should be listed on one page, customer reviews on another, your contact information on yet another, etc.

Your homepage should have very organized links to all these subpages so that the viewer can easily find what they're looking for. But it should not have a ton of information itself, or the viewer will become overwhelmed. Remember, if someone can't find what they need fast, they'll leave and go somewhere else.

SEO for Your Local Business Website

SEO stands for search engine optimization. It's the process of optimizing a website to rank it higher in the search engines. Because even if you have the best site in the world, it doesn't mean squat if nobody visits it.

Before we start going into more detail on SEO, it's important to note that SEO is a long term project. Depending on your industry and location, it can take 3 to 6 months just to see any improvement in ranking, and a year or more to reach your goal. Therefore, if you're going to "try" SEO or hire a SEO company for a month or two and then give up because you didn't see any results, don't even bother. It's just going to be a waste of time and money for you.

If you're going to stick with it, SEO can really pay off big time in the long run. For example, I did some research on the keyword "Houston chiropractor" using the Google Keyword Tool:

Your Website - Your Piece of the Internet

https://adwords.google.com/o/KeywordTool

The keyword has an estimated 6.6k monthly searches, while the approximate CPC (cost per click) is $6.52. What this means is that if you are advertising on Google's pay-per-click ad platform, you can expect to pay about $6.52 per click. Take a look at our screenshot of the Google Keyword Tool below:

Keyword	Competition	Global Monthly Searches	Local Monthly Searches	Ad Share	Google Search Network	Search Share	Approximate CPC (Search)	Local Search Trends	Extracted From Webpage
houston chiropractor	High	6,600	6,600	-	-	-	$6.52		-

Save all — Keyword ideas (225) — 1 - 100 of 225

Keyword	Competition	Global Monthly Searches	Local Monthly Searches	Ad Share	Google Search Network	Search Share	Approximate CPC (Search)	Local Search Trends
houston chiropractors	High	5,400	5,400	-	-	-	$6.17	
chiropractors in houston	High	5,400	5,400	-	-	-	$6.33	
chiropractors houston tx	High	1,300	1,300	-	-	-	$5.95	
chiropractor houston	High	6,600	6,600	-	-	-	$6.12	
chiropractor in houston	High	6,600	6,600	-	-	-	$6.75	
chiropractic houston	High	6,600	6,600	-	-	-	$6.73	
chiropractor houston texas	High	1,300	1,300	-	-	-	$5.94	
houston tx chiropractor	High	1,600	1,600	-	-	-	$5.39	
houston tx chiropractors	High	1,300	1,300	-	-	-	$5.64	

Let's break this down even further.

According to SEOmoz, over 85% of all searchers won't click advertisements. They'll go straight down to the organic results section. There are many theories on why this happens, but the most logical one is that people are naturally going to be a bit suspicious of ads.

Now obviously, the higher up your site is ranked on the organic search results, the more traffic you will get. Of the 85% who don't click on ads, 40% 50% of them will click on the first organic result. To keep it simple and conservative, let's just say that 25% of all searchers will end up clicking the first result.

For our Houston chiropractor example, that's roughly 1650 monthly clicks on your website (25% of the

6.6k total monthly searches) if you rank #1. If you were paying Google for each one of those clicks, you'd expect to pay them $10,758 per month!

In comparison, even the most expensive SEO firm will not charge you more than a few thousand dollars per month. You just need to be patient because as stated earlier, SEO does take time to start working.

All this is not even considering the multitudes of other related keywords you can target concurrently. If you look at the screenshot again, you'll see a short list of other keywords provided by Google which are similar to the main keyword. Keywords like "Houston chiropractors", "chiropractors in Houston", etc, represent other search terms potential customers could be typing in to find a local chiropractor. Just imagine how much business you would get if you could rank #1 for 5 or even 10 keywords.

SEO Basics

Proper SEO has two facets - on-site optimization and off-site optimization. On-site optimization is far by the easier component. It involves changes you can make to your actual website to make it more search engine friendly.

Here are the tasks I recommend:

1. Properly Optimize Your META Tags

META tags are information snippets found between the **<head>** and **</head>** tags on your website's HTML source. They include your website's title, description, and keywords. For example:

<head>
<title>Chiropractor Houston - Voted Top 10 Best

Chiropractor in Houston!**</title>**
<meta name="description" content="Relieve back pain and visit West Houston Chiropractor voted Top 10 Best. Physical Therapy and complete pain management specialist. Back pain relieved often on first visit." **/>**
<meta name="keywords" content="chiropractor, relieve back pain, back pain, chiropractic, back pain remedies, physical therapy, pain relief, pain management, pain management clinics, lower left back pain, lower back pain therapy, lower back pain causes, neck pain treatment" **/>**
</head>

The META tags above are from the #1 ranked website for the keyword "Houston chiropractor". The bolded text denotes HTML tags that you don't have to change.

The title is the most important component of your on-site SEO efforts. Most local businesses just put their business name as the title. That's not a good idea because people who don't know you are not going to search for you by name. They are much more likely to search for you by industry and location.

Notice how the first keyword in this website's title is "Chiropractor Houston", and it also features the keyword "Chiropractor in Houston" near the end. Nowhere in the title does it say what the clinic is actually called. The webmaster has done his keyword research and knows what people are actually searching for.

The description is not as important as the title for SEO purposes, but you'll want to include your main keyword here as well as add some other related keywords.

In our example, the description has the keywords "physical therapy", "pain management", and "back pain", which are all related to chiropractic care. In addition, the description does show up below your title in the search engine results (see example below), and some viewers do read them when deciding what website to visit. Even though they are a small percentage, you'll still want to cater to them regardless.

Chiropractor Houston - Voted Top 10 Best Chiropractor in Houston!
www.cesak**chiropractic**.com/
Relieve back pain and visit West **Houston Chiropractor** voted Top 10 Best. Physical therapy and complete pain management specialist. Back pain ...

Keywords are the least important of all. Search engines place little to no emphasis on their SEO value, mainly because they were abused to death in the past. I suggest that you don't skip it altogether, but just add your main target keyword and a few other related ones here, including your business name.

I'm assuming here that you are following my advice from earlier and you are building your local business website to include all the suggested components. Each of your pages should have plenty of relevant information, particularly on your homepage and industry specific pages. Ideally, each subpage of your site should target one keyword you want to be found for.

So if you are a chiropractor in Houston and you want to target the keyword "Houston chiropractor" primarily, your main page should feature a related article that's between 500 and 750 words. You can introduce yourself, your company and your main services. Try to use your main keyword in this article 7-8 times. Also, use titles and subtitles to split up your content and fit the keyword in them. For our chiropractor example, we can have the following:

Title: Are You Struggling With Pain? Experienced Houston Chiropractor At Your Service

Subtitle 1: Choosing the Right Houston Chiropractor

Subtitle 2: What Can a Houston Chiropractor Do For You?

Subtitle 3: Call a Houston Chiropractor Now and Put an End to the Pain

Now, you have already used the keyword 4 times. You just need to sprinkle it in a few more times in the paragraphs following the title and subtitles. By writing these first, you've also conveniently set up an outline for yourself. As you can guess, it'd be pretty easy for a chiropractor to expand on these topics.

Once you have the article written, it's time to format it the way search engines like. You already know that in order to help search engines learn what your content is about, you have to use your keyword a good number of times in your article. But that alone is not enough. You also have to emphasize it in various ways using HTML tags:

- Heading 1 - **\<h1>\</h1>**
- Heading 2 - **\<h2>\</h2>**
- Heading 3 - **\<h3>\</h3>**
- Bold - ****
- Italic - ****
- Underline - **\<u>\</u>**

Simply use the title and subtitles you created for the headings. Your title can be heading 1, your first subtitle would use heading 2, and so on. If you have more than 2 subtitles, you can always reuse heading 3 as many times as needed. Here are the chiropractor title and subtitles from earlier embedded in correct tags:

Title: <h1>Are You Struggling With Pain? Experienced Houston Chiropractor At Your Service**</h1>**
Subtitle 1: <h2>Choosing the Right Houston Chiropractor**</h2>**
Subtitle 2: <h3>What Can a Houston Chiropractor Do For You?**</h3>**
Subtitle 3: <h3>Call a Houston Chiropractor Now and Put an End to the Pain**</h3>**

Your keyword also must be bolded, italicized and underlined **on separate occasions** throughout your content. This should be easy if you followed my advice and used your keyword 7-8 times. Don't use all 3 modifiers at once, and don't use any on the keywords found in your headings.

Each page should also contain an image related to the content, with an alt tag that includes your keyword. This is what the HTML code looks like:

<img src="IMG URL" **alt=""**>

In between the bolded quotes is where you would put your image's alternate text. This text shows up if you mouse over the image, and it will replace the image entirely if a viewer has disabled images in his browser settings. Search engines use this text to determine what the image is of, since they obviously can't "see" it.

By following the guidelines above, your website will be more optimized than 99% of all local business websites out there. Below I've listed some additional steps you can take if time permits. Just be sure not to compromise readability if you decide to implement them:

- Use your keyword in the first and last sentences of your main content. Your title, which already contains your keyword, should be your first sentence, so in reality you only have to worry about fitting your keyword into the last sentence.

- Create a link to another related page on your website (internal link) using your keyword. This can be difficult because you're likely only going to have one page about any given topic. Do this only when the situation presents itself.

- Create a link to an authority website (external link), using your keyword. This is also situational, because in most cases, you don't want your visitors to leave your site and go somewhere else, so use this method sparingly. There are a lot of authority sites you can link to, and I personally like Wikipedia because it has an article on basically any topic you can imagine. About.com is a good one as well.

As a reminder, always remember that you are creating these pages for both search engines and people. Sometimes it can be pretty difficult to balance the two. Do your best to squeeze your keyword into your website a good number of times while keeping it easily readable overall.

2. Create and Upload a Google XML Sitemap

A sitemap is basically a document that tells search engines how your website is structured and how individual pages are interlinked. For example, it will tell search engines that your main page contains links to many other internal pages, and search engines will in turn interpret your main page as the hub of your website. Similarly, when two internal pages are linked together, search engines will assume that they are related in some way.

A sitemap's primary function is to help search engines index all of your pages properly. Your website will still get indexed without a sitemap, but it'll take longer. Google in particular loves sitemaps, which is enough reason to create one. To do so, visit the website below and follow the instructions:

http://xmlsitemap.com/create-sitemap/

As you can see, it's a very easy process. The website will do all the work for you, and all you have to do is download the resulting XML file and upload it to the root folder of your website.

Ideally, you should update your sitemap every time you add or delete a page on your website in order to notify search engines that changes have occurred. Or, at the very least, update it after you make major site revisions.

3. Add Privacy Policy, Terms of Service (ToS), and Disclaimer Pages to Your Website

Google and others search engines like to see these three pages. These documents protect you as the website owner should someone decide to sue for any reason. You do not have to hire a lawyer to draft up these documents. You can find free templates for all of them online, which you can then alter to your needs.

Off-site SEO

While on-site SEO involves factors you have complete control over, off-site SEO isn't nearly as simple. When you have a lot of great relevant content on your website and everything has been optimized perfectly, search engines now know exactly what your website is about and how valuable your information is. This by itself will earn you a lot of credibility, and, depending on the level of competition, a high spot in the search engines as well.

But the fact of the matter is that a lot of local niches are fiercely competitive and filled with websites who offer great information just like yours. How do you differentiate yourself?

While nobody knows Google's exact ranking algorithm, over time SEO experts have collectively attained an impressive level of understanding on how sites are ranked. For simplicity's sake, let's pretend that Google is holding a popularity contest for all the websites in its database, and your website is participating.

When someone likes your website, they can...

- Click the Facebook Like button on your site
- Give your site a Google thumbs up (Google +1)
- Tweet about your website
- Share your link on a social bookmarking site
- Post your link to their blog
- Link to your website from their site

And so on. Your visitors have many fast and easy options to react in some way after reading your content.

We can split up the different reactions into two categories - social signals and backlinks.

Social signals are your Facebook likes, Google +1's, Tweets, social bookmarks, forum posts, blog comments, etc. They are open and available for everyone to use. It'd be extremely difficult to find an Internet user in the United States who doesn't have any social networking accounts and doesn't participate in a single online community.

Backlinks, on the other hand, are incoming links to your website from other websites. Most of your visitors will not have their own websites, so this method is pretty much restricted to webmasters and bloggers.

Backlinks used to play a huge role in determining search engine rankings, and while they still matter a great deal today, their effect is slowly waning. Search engines are starting to favor social signals instead as they realize that not everyone has a website or even a blog.

Most people rely exclusively on social networking to share what they find on the Internet today, be it a funny video, interesting news, or useful information. Remember, the sole purpose of a successful search engine is to provide the most relevant content to its users, and to achieve this goal it must take social signals from the masses into consideration. In general (and there are exceptions), the more social network mentions a website has, the more credibility that site earns with the search engines.

The search engine's logic is easy to understand. Let's take the hypothetical websites of two fictitious Houston chiropractors and compare them:

- Dr. Smith has 248 Google plus ones (+1's), 312

Tweets mentioning his website, and 145 Facebook users linking to him.
- Dr. Green has 52 Google +1's, 98 Tweets, and 85 Facebook links.

Who, in the eyes of a search engine, is the "better" chiropractor? The answer is clearly Dr. Smith. Note that this has nothing to do with who's *actually* a more qualified doctor in real life, because the search engine obviously has no way of knowing. That's why it bases its rankings on overall public sentiment.

This is a very rudimentary example, of course. In reality, many more social signals are factored in. Add your on-site optimization and backlinks to the mix, as well as possible hidden metrics, and you end up with a super complex algorithm search engines use to determine rankings.

In many cases, a social signal can also be considered a backlink and vice versa. For example, if someone writes this Tweet: "Dr. Smith got rid of my leg pain completely! If you need a chiropractor, here's his website: ...", he is mentioning you on a social media platform while also linking back to your website.

Links from Facebook status updates, social bookmarks, and to a lesser degree even forum posts all fit into this category as well. Facebook likes and Google +1's, on the other hand, would be considered pure social signals since the participants aren't actively posting links to your site.

However, as I alluded to earlier, it's not just about sheer numbers. Although unlikely, it is possible that Dr. Green's website outranks Dr. Smith's, even if they both have perfectly optimized websites and no other backlinks.

This is where off-site SEO becomes more difficult to understand - the fact is that not all backlinks and social signals are equal in value to a search engine.

Suppose Dr. Smith's Google +1's, Facebook links, and Tweets are all from brand new accounts created for the purpose of inflating these numbers. Search engine bots can easily detect such artificial links and ignore them when determining a website's rank. Someone new to SEO may try something like this and end up with miserable results.

Or, maybe the +1's, links, and Tweets are all from real users, people like you and me. In this case it would be difficult for Dr. Green to outrank Dr. Smith. But believe it or not, he still can. If Dr. Green is a well known expert in his field of chiropractic care, and many of his social signals come from other authority figures in the industry, then he will have more credibility with the search engines and therefore rank higher.

Below are some factors that affect how search engines determine the value of your backlinks and social signals:

Activity Level of Social Media Users

As mentioned before, social signals (such as Google +1's and Facebook likes) from active, established users are worth more than ones from new or inactive users.

PageRank of Websites Linking to You

A backlink from a website with higher Google PageRank (PR) is worth more than one from a low PR site. Each site is ranked by Google on a PR scale of 0 to 10. PR10 is reserved for the most popular websites on the Internet, such as Google itself, Apple, Facebook, Twitter, and so on, while PR0 sites are either new or basically unknown. A website's PageRank is updated by Google periodically and therefore will fluctuate over time. You can check the PageRank for any URL using this tool:

http://www.prchecker.info

Generally speaking, the higher a page's PR is, the more difficult it is to get a backlink from it. A blog that's PR4 or 5 is likely to have a readership count in the tens of thousands, for instance, and it's much harder to get the owner's attention. This is why a link from such a website provides more value than a PR0 site nobody visits.

Also, if you're building links from any page of a website that's not the homepage, be aware that the internal page's PR is likely going to be lower than the root domain's PR. For example, Twitter.com is a PR10 domain, but individual account pages are mostly PR0, unless the account belongs to someone with tons of followers (for example, Oprah's Twitter profile page is ranked PR7).

So if you have a link from a PR0 page, the SEO effect will be minimal even if that page's root domain is PR10. But the high PR root will still help a little bit, and that link will be worth more than a backlink from a page with a PR0 root domain.

Relevancy of Backlinks

A relevant backlink is worth more than an unrelated one. For example, if you're a chiropractor, a link from a pain management website is worth more than one from a site about sports betting.

Content on Sites Linking to You

A backlink from a website with fewer outbound links (OBL) is worth more than one with tons of OBL.

The logic here is that sites with a high number of OBL are considered to be "link farms" by search engines. These are pages that are usually spammed to death by people building backlinks to their websites, as a webmaster is unlikely to populate his own page with a bunch of unrelated outgoing links.

Building Backlinks

Before we get down to the nitty-gritty of link building, first be aware that you can't "build" social signals. Think about Google +1's, for example. The only way to increase your website's +1 count yourself is to create a bunch of Google accounts, log into each, and click the +1 button on your site. Not surprisingly, Google doesn't like this. As demonstrated in our chiropractor example earlier, fake social signals are easily detected by search engines and ignored for the purpose of ranking. In due time, those fake accounts will be deleted and their +1's on Dr. Smith's website will be removed as well.

As such, social signals must come naturally and from real people. You can certainly ask your friends, family, colleagues and customers to +1 your page, but that's about as far as you can go.

Now, let's go over some simple ways you can build backlinks to your website:

Blogging

Create accounts on the most popular blogging platforms and include links from your posts back to your website.

This is one of the most effective off-site SEO methods by far, but also the most time consuming. High

PR blogging platforms are trusted by search engines, and by extension, individual accounts also benefit from their reputation.

There are 50 or so well-known blogging platforms you can sign up with. However, each account will require some work. Don't compose a single post containing a link to your website and then promptly abandon the account. There are two reasons for this. One, many of these blogging platforms have been spammed to death by people who're just looking for quick backlinks, so they now employ moderators to check what the new members are posting. So if your first post consists of nothing but a link to your site, you can bet that your account will be deleted in no time and you've lost that backlink. Two, search engines do take the content surrounding any outgoing link on a webpage into consideration. If they find little to no related information, the value of that link diminishes.

To address these two issues, you must create relevant content for your blogs just like you did for your website. Then, the content should be optimized in a similar fashion as described before in the on-site SEO section. Ideally, in order to get past strict moderators, the first post should not contain any links. Wait a week or two and then make your second post, where you can finally add in your link. Be sure to use the keyword you're targeting as the anchor text (clickable text in a hyperlink).

The blog posts do not have to be as long as the articles you write for your website. 300-400 words per post will be enough. Of course, it's still a lot of work to create 2 short articles for each blogging platform. Take your time. Again, SEO is a marathon, not a sprint. Start with the 5 most important platforms:

- http://blogger.com (Google owns this)
- http://wordpress.com
- http://tumblr.com
- http://squidoo.com
- http://weebly.com

A full list of sites you can create blogs on can be found at http://getinternetexposure.com/blogging.

Social Networking

Create links to your website from your social networking accounts, such as Facebook, Twitter, and LinkedIn. You can add these links to both your personal accounts as well as accounts created for your local business. Be sure to keep these accounts active.

Video Marketing

Create videos about your business, upload them to video sharing sites, and add a link to your website in each video's description. (For more details on video marketing, see chapter 6.)

Post on Forums

Visit forums related to your industry, participate in the discussions, and post your link when appropriate. Keep in mind that forums have been subjected to serious spam in the past few years and most have adopted a zero-tolerance policy. Read the rules for each individual forum carefully. Some will let you post links as long as they're relevant to the topic at hand, others only allow links in your signature, while few will not accept links at all.

Even forums that allow links will often require you to have a certain number of posts before you receive that privilege. However, with your expertise in the field, you should be able to build your post count and establish your credibility fairly quickly by helping other members. As a chiropractor, for instance, you can comment on a thread about pain management exercises and include a link back to your website for more information, provided that you have a page set up on that subject matter.

Answer Questions

Visit Yahoo Answers (http://answers.yahoo.com), find questions related to your field of expertise, and include a link back to your website with each response. It helps to establish your authority when you answer questions. For example, state how many years you've been a chiropractor.

Comment on Blogs

Find blog posts related to your industry and add useful, relevant comments. Mention or quote something from the post so that the author knows you actually read it. Add to the discussion; don't just say "very interesting read" or "I loved how insightful your article was". Generic comments such as these have been abused by spammers and will most likely not get approved by the author.

Do not add any links into the comment field. Most blogs are set up to automatically reject such comments. To include a link to your website from a blog comment, we must take a different approach. When you post a blog comment you'll be asked to fill out 4 fields - name, email, website URL, and comment. In the "Name" field, be sure to use the keyword you're targeting, such as "Houston chiropractor", and not your real name. This field will actually serve as the anchor text that will link to the URL you specify.

Social Bookmarking

Create social bookmarks to your website. Social bookmarking is basically a way for people to organize and share their favorite links with others. Use the keyword you're targeting in the title of each bookmark, and write a short description of what your website is about. Include as many secondary keywords in your description as you can.

There are thousands of social bookmarking websites out there. Some examples include Delicious, Digg, and Reddit. You don't need to (nor is it even possible) post to them all. Start with the 50 most popular sites and go from there:

http://getinternetexposure.com/socialbookmarks

How fast should you build links? Well, let me backtrack a bit and explain why you even need to ask this question in the first place. Yes, it does matter and it is possible to build too many, too quickly. It may surprise you, but the search engines don't like you. Because believe it or not, by doing SEO work on your website, you are attempting to manipulate the system.

Essentially, you're serving up what search engines want to see so that they'll rank you higher. You're artificially adding "votes" to your website in this popularity contest. This works directly against the ultimate goal of search engines, which is to provide the most relevant results for each search. They obviously would prefer all backlinks to be built naturally and by real people who enjoyed your site so much that they just had to tell the world. In that case, the search results they display for each query would reflect true public sentiment.

You might be thinking to yourself now that SEO is an unethical practice. Most SEO experts would not admit this, but yes, at its core, SEO is pure exploitation of a robot's (search engine's) limitations. Remember, search engines don't know whether your content is truly good or not. Sure, it can scan your pages, find the most prevalent keywords used and determine with high accuracy what your website is about, but that's it. It's not going to be able to tell if that content is helpful to people.

However, SEO is an absolute requirement if you want to gain more business from your website. There's just no way around this, no matter what your personal feelings regarding the matter are. For one thing, your top competitors are doing SEO, guaranteed. In fact, I'm willing to bet that less than 0.01% of all websites found on the top 3 search results for any local search term got there organically.

Here's my stance on the moral dilemma at hand: if you provide excellent content that is beneficial to your target audience, then to me there's nothing unethical about giving yourself a push to the top. That's why search engines tolerate SEO to a certain extent. But there are always people who will take any shortcut they can find in their attempt to get websites ranked high without much good content. These are the sites search engines really want to penalize.

Google, for example, frequently releases algorithm updates that are designed to find and penalize sites who faked their way to the top. The last two such updates were facetiously dubbed "Panda" and "Penguin." But as explained earlier, since Google cannot empirically judge a website's content, it must dish out penalties based on a website's SEO activity. This is why I constantly reiterate that you cannot expect quick results from SEO.

See, with the right software, a SEO firm can create

thousands of backlinks to your website per day. But doing so throws up a huge red flag for all search engines to see. It's extremely unnatural, especially for a local business website, to suddenly go viral and gain thousands of incoming links in a day. When Google finds these links, it's going to know instantly that you're doing some hardcore backlinking, and your site will be penalized accordingly.

So in order for you to successfully increase your website's ranking using SEO, you must take it slow and make all your activities appear as natural as possible. Get backlinks of all types and from as many different websites as you can. Don't spend months only getting backlinks from forums, and then switch over to blogs for the next few months. Search engines are experts at detecting patterns, so don't let yourself fall into one. Your backlinking activities should be random and chaotic. Add a blog post today, forum link tomorrow, social bookmark the day after, and so on.

With every Google update, 1 to 2% of all websites are negatively affected in the rankings. Many of these sites have great content, but messed up somewhere along the way while building links. Don't become part of that statistic.

That being said, it's getting harder and harder to dodge the Google algorithm update bullet. Bots are becoming smarter and programmed to find more SEO footprints than ever before. Just keeping up with the list of daily Google changes is a full time job. In fact, by the time you read this book, some information might be outdated already.

To save yourself some major headaches, I would suggest that you hire a competent SEO firm. Even if you only have the budget to outsource one task, this is undoubtedly your best choice. Trying to keep up with all the curveballs search engines throw at you while still running your local business is next to impossible. Plus, manual link building is one of the most tedious and time consuming tasks you can subject yourself to. And you might have zero results to show for it (or even get penalized) if you make one tiny mistake.

A good SEO firm can get your website ranked in the shortest time possible, while obeying all the rules laid out by search engines. With each algorithm change, SEO specialists will work hard to formulate new strategies. They also have access to many tools that can automate some of the more time consuming tasks and pass on the savings to you.

As a side note, beware of SEO companies that advertise manual link building as a benefit and charge you a premium for it. First of all, search engines do not know whether a link is built manually or by a software program. Thus, it makes absolutely no sense to manually perform a task that can be automated to achieve the same result. Unscrupulous companies can easily claim that they're building links manually, while in reality using a software program like everyone else, and you'd never know the difference.

In conclusion, whether you decide to outsource your SEO work or not, always remember that the two core concepts to successful link building will never change. You will always need:

- Backlinks that are built gradually over time
- Many types of backlinks from different websites

One last thing I want to mention is that off-site

factors (social signals and backlinks) matter far more than on-site optimization (META tags, content, etc.) when it comes to ranking high in the search engines. As a fun little test, we were able to rank a website on the first page for a completely unrelated keyword. That keyword was not mentioned anywhere on the site, so the high ranking can be attributed completely to backlinks using that unrelated keyword as the anchor text.

So, let's go back to our popularity contest analogy. Suppose you've been nominated to be the prom queen in high school. You can wear a pretty dress, get a cool tattoo, or style your hair to be more fashionable. Just like on-site SEO, these are factors you have complete control over. You might garner a few extra votes by attracting more attention with your new look, but your influence is going to be negligible, especially since the other nominees (your competitors) will be doing the same. The votes from your peers (off-site SEO) will ultimately determine whether you win or not.

3. Mobile Website "Exposure On-the-Go"

It is estimated that by 2014, nearly all phones in use in the United States will be smartphones. AT&T and other carriers have begun to push their smart devices and data plans onto existing customers who are still using "old-school" phones. As of this writing, there are already 98 million smartphones in use in the U.S., and this number is projected to double by 2014.

The use of desktop computers continues to decline as more and more consumers switch entirely to using their phones. After all, a smartphone is more convenient and can cater to most web-based needs of a typical person. It's easy to see why smartphones are quickly rising to the top in our 21st century on-the-go culture - with affordable data plans, a smartphone can be used to access the Internet from just about anywhere.

This is why having a mobile optimized version of your business website is so important. People are going to be viewing your site on tiny smartphone screens, and while they can still load the "regular" version that's meant to be seen on a large computer monitor, it'll be difficult to navigate and the text will be nearly impossible to read.

Here are two examples of sites which are not mobile optimized:

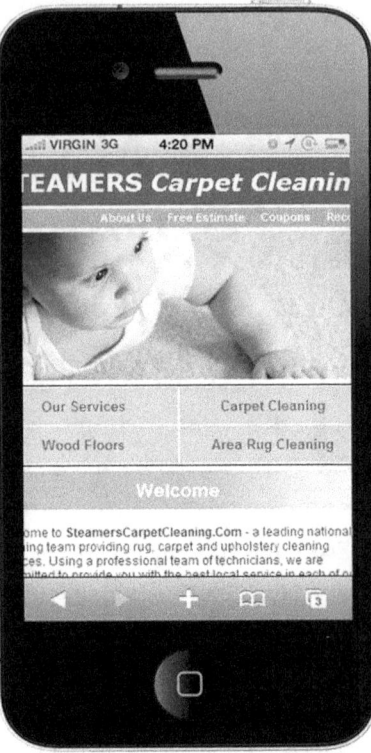

By the way, I'm not picking on these websites. They just happened to be good examples of sites that look great on a computer monitor, but not on a smartphone. In both cases, the text is way too small to read unless you zoom in. Once you do, you then must scroll to the right and back left constantly to read full lines of text. At best, this is an annoyance. At worst, busy and impatient consumers won't even bother with you. Never forget that they likely have tons of options available no matter what service provider they're looking for.

As a side note, it's worth pointing out that any Flash content on your website will not display on the iOS, the operating system for Apple devices. iOS has an approximate market share of 30% in the United States, which is reason enough to not use Flash. Plus, Flash can also cause problems for people with slower Internet connections.

The number one objective of a mobile friendly website is to be easily readable on mobile devices. To achieve this goal, your mobile site must follow these guidelines:

- Scrolling should be limited to up and down only.
- Your business name and a click-to-call button must be highly visible on the homepage. This will make it super easy for customers to contact you at the touch of a button. Note that just using your phone number will work here as well. Smartphones will automatically convert it to a clickable link to call.
- Keep the text to a minimum. While it's okay to talk about yourself and your business on the homepage of your regular website, it'll be nothing but a distraction on your mobile site. At most, you should only include a short description of your business and set up a separate "About Us" page for the rest.
- If a potential customer is on your mobile site, he's usually looking for specific information. If he can't find it within a few seconds, chances are that he'll leave. Create a clean, straightforward menu system on your homepage that's easy to navigate.
- Users visiting your site on smartphones should automatically be redirected to the mobile-optimized version. There are many free scripts available on the

Internet that'll detect what device a user is accessing your site from and redirect him accordingly.

- People who are out and about using their 3G/4G service will most likely not have a super fast connection. Keep your mobile site simple and to the point. Remember, nobody is on there to admire how pretty it is. Your logo and a few small images here and there are fine, but don't overdo it. If your site takes too long to load, many viewers will leave and never look back.

Below are two examples of mobile-optimized websites:

As you can tell, these sites are clean and uncluttered; they are much easier to read and navigate through compared to our first two examples.

To make sure that a prospective customer will find exactly what he's looking for, below is a list of subpages I advise you to include on your mobile site:

- Hours of operation
- Basic list of services/products
- Address, map, and driving directions
- News and updates
- Customer reviews
- An "About Us" page
- A link to your regular (full) website
- Images and videos (optional)
- Coupons and special offers (if applicable)

Do not cram all this information onto the homepage. That would not only overwhelm visitors but also make any specific piece of information very difficult to find. Create a subpage for each of these topics. Customer A may only be wondering if you're still open at 10PM, while Customer B just wants to see if you're currently running specials. By splitting up the information onto separate pages and linking to them from the main page, both customers in this scenario can find what they need in a matter of seconds.

All in all, a mobile site is really just an extension of your regular website. You don't have to worry about doing SEO work for it, as your main site's rank carries over when someone conducts a search on their smartphone.

One last topic I want to cover is the URL choices for your mobile site. Currently the two most widely accepted formats are:

- http://**m**.domainname.com - the "m" here stands for mobile and is a subdomain.
- http://domainname.**mobi** - the word "mobi" is a TLD (top-level domain) extension similar to .com.

So let's say your domain name is GadgetsForSale.com. You can either set up the subdomain **http://m.GadgetsForSale.com**, which is free. Or, you can register a brand new domain name, **http://GadgetsForSale.mobi**, at a cost of around $20-30 per year. In both cases, you would then set up your mobile site on the chosen URL and, using a redirect script, send all visitors browsing from smartphones to it.

You might be wondering which choice is better. Well, mobile marketing experts have been debating this topic for years, and there's still no clear winner thus far. So I suggest that you simply do both. Set up your mobile site on the subdomain and redirect all traffic from the .mobi domain to it.

If your budget is low, it's certainly fine to start with just the subdomain.

4. Local Listings "e-Business Directories"

As mentioned before, approximately 20% of all search queries have local intent. Search engines recognize this and in response, they've implemented a section in the search results for listings of local businesses.

These listings do not appear for all search terms. For instance, if you were to search for something generic such as "sleep apnea" on Google, you won't see any local business listings. In this case, Google has used its internal algorithm to determine that the vast majority of people searching for "sleep apnea" are merely looking for information and not looking for local businesses. On the other hand, a keyword like "sleep apnea clinic" will trigger local listings, since it indicates a physical location.

Google will serve up relevant business listings once it has determined that your search has local intent. It can accomplish this in one of two ways. The first is by checking to see if there is a location modifier added to your search term. Examples include "chiropractor Houston" (screenshot on the following page), "Katy TX electrician", and "plumber in Houston Texas".

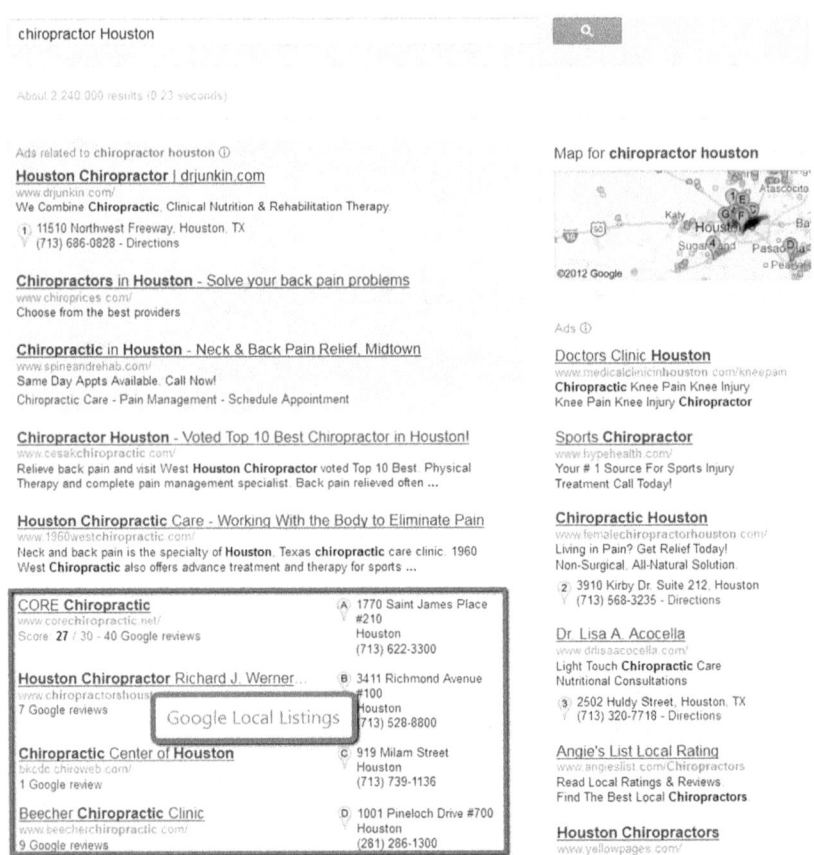

The second method is a bit more complicated. Basically, Google can detect your IP address and extrapolate your location from it. This is not always accurate, so Google allows you to manually set (or change) your location. With this information, Google no longer needs to see location modifiers with search terms in order to serve up local results. For example, I live in Cinco Ranch, which is a small neighborhood right outside of Houston, TX. The screenshot on the following page shows what I get when I just type in "chiropractor" on Google.

LOCAL LISTINGS - E-BUSINESS DIRECTORIES

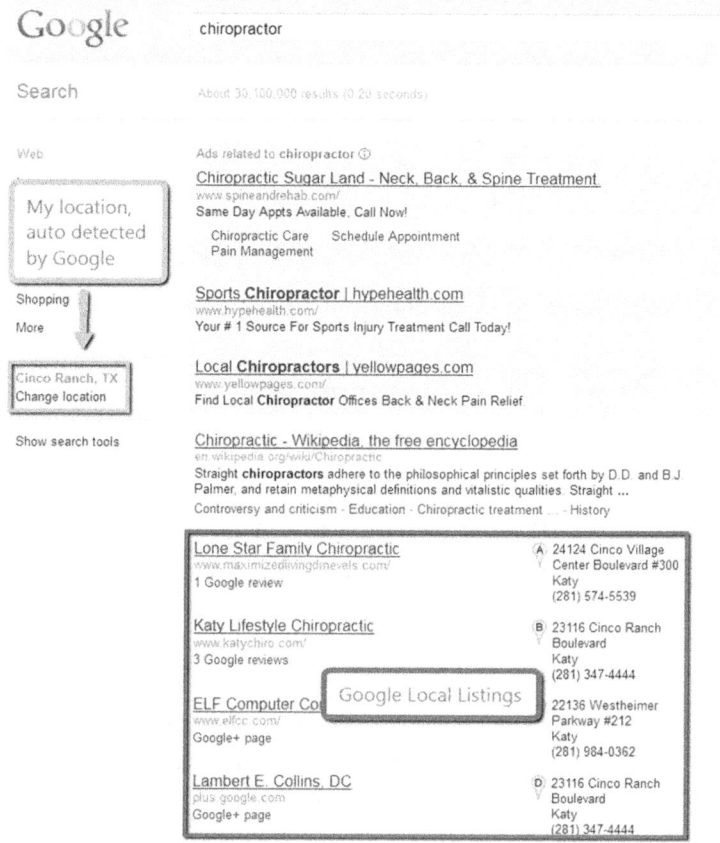

You can see why local listings are so powerful now. While it's probably not that difficult to rank your website for location specific search terms like "Cinco Ranch chiropractor", it would be incredibly hard to rank for just "chiropractor", because now you're competing against every site on the net about chiropractors.

On the other hand, since local listings get their own designated space on the search results, you're only competing against other local businesses.

There are many local listing sites you can sign up for, and you should join as many as possible. Here is a list of the most important ones to get you started:

- Google Local - http://www.google.com/places/
- Yelp - http://www.yelp.com/
- Yahoo Local - http://local.yahoo.com/
- Bing Local - http://www.bing.com/local/
- CitySearch - http://www.citysearch.com/
- ExpressUpdate - http://expressupdateusa.com/
- LocalEze - http://localeze.com/
- FourSquare - http://foursquare.com/business/
- SuperPages - http://superpages.com/
- Yellow Pages - http://yp.com/
- HotFrog - http://www.hotfrog.com/
- Best of the Web - http://botw.org/

The signup process is extremely easy and most sites offer step-by-step guidance. Some of them will already have listings for your local business populated with information obtained from other local listing sites and public records. You just need to claim these listings by verifying your ownership of the business either via telephone or mail.

When signing up, you'll be asked for vital information about your business (such as name, address, phone number, hours of operations, etc.) as well as photos. Follow these guidelines when creating your listings:

- Keep your information consistent across all local listing sites - especially your business name, address, and phone number. Local listing sites frequently syndicate information from each other, and conflicting data can cause duplicate listings or even result in a

LOCAL LISTINGS - E-BUSINESS DIRECTORIES

ranking penalty.

It's best to simply use your official business name, as in the exact name that appears on your business license or DBA. Do not abbreviate or substitute (for example, "&" is not treated the same as "and" on local listings).

- Make your listings as "full" as possible - provide everything the local listing sites ask for, even if it's optional. A description of your business, your website URL, accepted payment types, parking instructions (if your business is situated in a busy location with limited parking), hours of operation, and photos of your establishment are all crucial. The more information you have available on your local listings, the more credible you appear to prospective customers.

Based on their Google local listings alone, which of the two hair salons below are you more likely to choose?

1. TGF Hair Salon

No description, no photos, and no hours of operation listed. It looks like the owner just added the bare minimum information required and was done with it. (Screenshot on following page.)

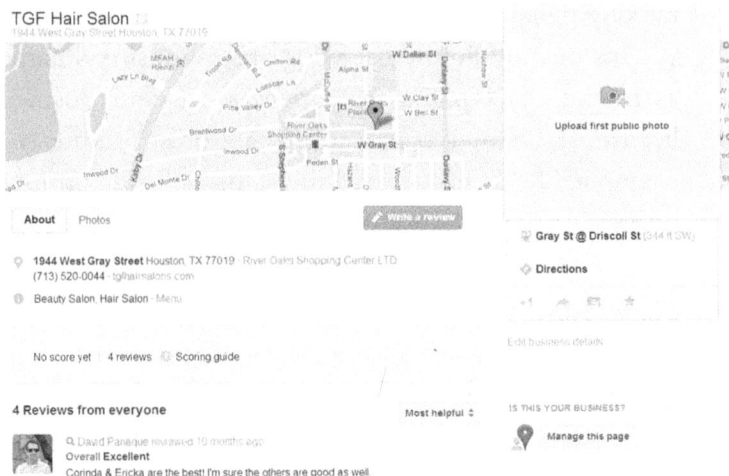

2. Monica Montalbano

Her listing includes a powerful personal statement as the description, beautiful pictures of her salon, and of course, hours of operation.

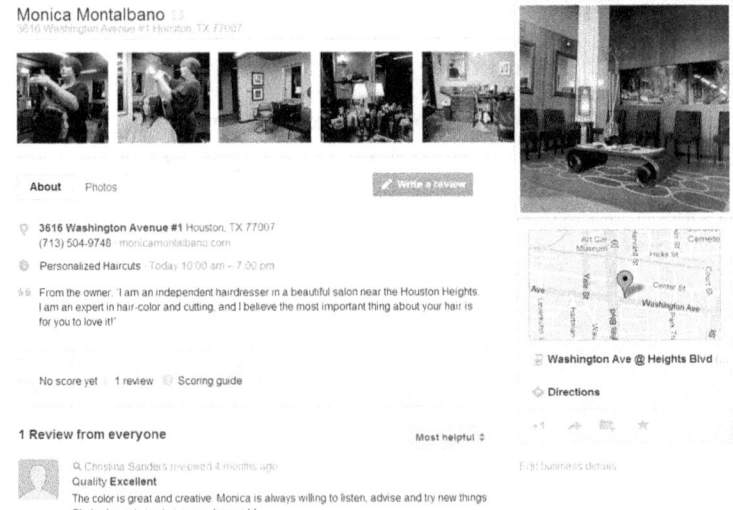

LOCAL LISTINGS - E-BUSINESS DIRECTORIES

While TGF appears to be a faceless corporation, you get the feeling that you already know Monica simply by reading her description. If you look at all her photos, you'll really get a sense of her style.

- Try to use keywords you're targeting in your description - but make sure it flows naturally. Some location specific keywords will sound awkward in a sentence, especially when the city or town name comes after the main keyword, such as "chiropractor Houston". In this case, do not force it. Just use both words separately (i.e. "I was rated the top **chiropractor** in the **Houston** area").

   You should also include as many secondary keywords as possible. In Monica's case, she included "salon", "Heights" (the neighborhood in Houston where her salon is located), "hair color", and "cutting" in her description, which are all related to her main keyword, "hairdresser Houston".

- Be patient when making changes - some local listing sites take very long to process them. Google is perhaps the slowest of them all, as most updates can take up to a week before they are reflected on your listing. Newly uploaded images may not appear for a month or more. The best advice I can give you is to double check and make sure that everything's correct when you first create the listing, so you don't have to worry about making too many revisions later down the road.

Ranking Your Listings

Like your website, your goal is to rank your local listings on page one of the search results for maximum exposure. This can be a lengthy process depending on how many competitors you are up against, and it's an entirely different beast from SEO.

Each listing's ranking depends on the following:

Citations

The number of citations you have is by far the most important factor. Citations are basically "mentions" of your local business on the world wide web. A citation often includes a link back to your website, but it's not required. As long as your business name and address are both listed on a site, then you've got a valid citation. This is why it's so crucial for you to keep all your information consistent, so local listing sites can easily find your citations.

You can get citations from a variety of different websites, including local listing sites obviously, local blogs and news portals, local business directories, and industry specific sites. To get you started, here's a comprehensive list of more than 100 websites you can get citations from:

http://getinternetexposure.com/citations

Don't go overboard with adding tons of citations every day. Like backlinks, too many citations too fast can actually hurt your rankings. 2-3 new ones per week is enough.

Reviews

In order to rank well, you need plenty of positive reviews on your local listings. Because this is such an extensive topic, I cover it at length in chapter 7.

Local Listings - e-Business Directories

Website Optimization

Ranking your local listings has a lot to do with how well optimized your website is and how many relevant local backlinks it has. Follow the guidelines laid out in chapter 2 and you'll have nothing to worry about. If you don't have time to fully optimize your website right now, then at least be absolutely sure to include your business NAP (name, address, phone number) on every page of your site.

There are many ways to get local backlinks, which are just links to your website from sites with a local focus. Here are some ideas:

- Add a citation from as many local business directories as you can find, and include your website URL on each.
- Join your local chamber of commerce and networking groups (such as BNI and RLI), and add your website URL on your profile pages.
- Contact local bloggers to see if you can write a post for them in exchange for a link back. Bloggers are always looking for new, fresh content, and you have helpful industry-specific information to offer (for example, if you're a personal trainer, you can offer bodybuilding tips).
- If you have a newsworthy story to tell, convince a local reporter to interview you. An article about your business on a local news websites will not only give you additional exposure, but provide a backlink to your website as well. For 109 tips on how to attract media attention, visit:
http://getinternetexposure.com/pr

You might be wondering whether you should focus on ranking your website or your local listings. The answer is that you must work on both simultaneously. In many cases, the ranking of your website affects the rankings of your local listings and vice versa. Together, the synergy between them will generate more business for you than each will on its own.

5. Social Media
"Keeping Up With the Times"

Social media is not a fad. In fact, it's the fastest growing sector on the Internet right now and will remain so in the foreseeable future. Occasionally, a new social media website will pop up to replace an older one, forcing it to slowly die out. For example, Facebook has pretty much made MySpace obsolete. However, the total number of social media users is increasing on a daily basis, and has been for years.

Facebook and Myspace are what I call the "do-it-all" social networks. They let you write posts, create links, upload videos/images, play games, and enjoy a myriad of other activities. Then, you have the more specialized social media sites like Twitter and Pinterest. Although Twitter has been adding additional functions to their platform, such as the ability to include images with tweets, it has not strayed far from the original 140-character tweeting system. Pinterest is a relatively new social network for uploading, sharing, and collecting images.

In this book, we're going to focus on Facebook and Twitter, the two largest and most important social networks for local businesses. Although we do want to keep an eye on Pinterest as it is gaining momentum extremely fast, its user count is still dwarfed by the two giants at the time of this writing.

Facebook

It's now more important than ever to have a Facebook fan page for your local business. 900 million people have Facebook accounts, and many of them are on it hours a day. It's hands down the best platform on which to build relationships with your customers, and it only takes a few minutes to set up. Just visit:

http://www.facebook.com/pages/create.php

Simply follow the instructions. Keep in mind that you'll need a Facebook personal account before you can create a page for your business.

So why do you need a Facebook fan page? Well, many business owners believe that word of mouth is the best advertising method out there. Facebook can take this method and put it on steroids. But first, you'll need to build a fan base. To do this you must add your Facebook URL to all of your promotional materials, website, and even physical assets in some cases. Always feature the Facebook logo along with your URL, because it's highly recognizable and attention grabbing. Here are some ideas on where you can include your fan page URL:

- Business cards
- Brochures
- Fliers
- Appointment cards
- Custom logo merchandise
- Signs

- Website
- Billboards
- Print advertisements
- Front door of your business
- Company vehicles

You can provide a small incentive for users to like your fan page. For example, periodic special offers only for Facebook fans. Make it a habit to casually tell customers (as they're checking out or waiting) about your fan page.

Over time your fan base will grow steadily. Don't try to rush it and don't be impatient. Just like SEO, social media marketing takes time.

Once you have some fans, start engaging them in conversation. Post to your fan page frequently. By this I don't mean spam your fans 10 times a day. Keep it reasonable, but post often enough so they don't forget that you exist. For local businesses, 3-5 times a week is ideal. There are always exceptions, of course. Let's say you're a retailer and it's the Christmas shopping season. Then you'll obviously want to post more often since you probably have a lot of deals going on.

If you are struggling to come up with topics to post about, here are some ideas:

- Industry related tips (Ex: If you're a personal trainer, how about fitness tips?)
- Discounts and special offers
- New service or product releases
- Other news and updates (Ex: If your store is closing temporarily for remodeling.)
- Customer testimonials

- New employee (Ex: "John is a new sales associate here; let's welcome him.")
- Holidays and other events (Ex: "Have a fun and safe Labor Day weekend!")
- Ask questions and conduct polls (Ex: "What's your favorite type of pie?")
- Random chitchat (Ex: "It's almost Friday! Are you as excited as we are?")

As you can see, there are a lot of things you can talk about with your fans. Don't always advertise your company, because your fans will get tired of that quickly. You want to be human and talk about daily life as well. You can always sneak in a self pitch here and there, just don't overdo it. Only 1 out of every 5 updates should be an ad.

Also, include pictures, videos, and links whenever you can. Don't just post text updates over and over again. Not only do posts with media stand out a lot more, they're far more interesting. So in the new employee example, you can add a photo of John along with the update. Videos are harder to come by, but if you have a webcam or video camera, you can simply record yourself talking if you happen to have a longer update to give your fans.

For example, if your company is starting a refer-a-friend program, you can explain how the program works, what the compensation will be, and so on. You'll be able to go into more depth on a video than in a written status update. People don't want to read a wall of text, but they will watch a 1-2 minute video, no problem.

You can also upload any video testimonials you may have recorded, as well as informative industry related videos. Going back to our chiropractor example, fans of a chiropractor will enjoy videos on healthy diets, stress relief exercises, pain management, and so on. Once you have these videos made and uploaded to Facebook, you can add them to your website as well.

Now, back to what I was saying about Facebook facilitating your word of mouth advertising efforts. Again, let's use the chiropractor example. As a chiropractor, you help your patients reduce and eliminate pain naturally through spinal adjustments and exercises. There are two ways a happy customer can help spread the word about you on Facebook:

1. By posting about you directly

Even an update as inconspicuous as "Off to the chiropractor" could help you out. Remember, Facebook is all about conversation. A friend of the poster can always ask something like "Hey, does a chiropractor really help with the pain? I'm having back pain myself", or "Who do you go to? I'm looking for a chiropractor".

If you are good at what you do and your clients are happy, they'll take such opportunities to refer new business to you.

On the other hand, a happy client can straight up recommend you in a status update. For instance, he can post "Back pain finally gone, thanks to Dr. Smith!" This doesn't happen too often, but providing top-notch service certainly increases your chances.

In both of these cases, if your business has a Facebook fan page, your clients can easily link to it. You'll get more fans this way, too. If you don't have a fan page, then your client has to go find your website or phone number, which is too much of a hassle for most people.

2. By replying to friends' posts

People ask for recommendations all the time on Facebook, because they trust their friends. So if one of your client's friends posted "My back is killing me. Who knows a good chiropractor?", you can score a recommendation right there.

Twitter

Most of what you need to do on Facebook also applies to Twitter. Be aware that you are far more limited as to what you can post. 140 characters don't go that far, especially if you need to add links. Do your best to truncate longer posts down to one tweet each, and avoid splitting one story over several tweets.

One thing worth noting about Twitter is that people can subscribe to your tweets and receive them on their smartphones. This can be extremely powerful because we all know how glued to smartphones people are nowadays.

Keep posting relevant and interesting content as well as offer great deals, and you'll get more subscribers. You can send out exclusive one-day or same-day deals to reward subscribers, and pitch this as an incentive to follow you on Twitter. This method works best for restaurants because everyone has to eat everyday. This means you can send out a Tweet like "10% off of your total bill, TODAY only" and possibly get some interested customers. If you're a chiropractor, on the other hand, sending out a Tweet like "10% off of your adjustment, TODAY only" won't work as well because people don't typically get that kind of service done on a whim.

Your Tweets don't have to be different from your Facebook posts, as long as their length and format comply with Twitter's rules. In fact, whatever you post on one *should* also be on the other, besides the platform specific special deals. Some of your customers will be a fan of you on Facebook as well as your follower on Twitter, but most prefer one or the other. Informing customers that you have different deals for users of each site can help persuade more of them to join you on both.

Again, don't spam. Spamming is a great way to lose subscribers and followers. You can even get your account banned in extreme cases.

Engage Your Customers

Both Facebook and Twitter allow customers to contact you directly. This is a plus for them because many people don't want to email or call. It's just easier to post a message on Facebook or send a Tweet when they're on these sites all the time anyway.

You'll want to reply to every message you receive, even if they are just comments that typically don't require responses. If you receive a compliment, say thanks. If you get a question, answer it. Your customers want to know you're active on these sites. They want to know that you didn't basically abandon the page shortly after creating it. Yes, it is a lot of work, but it'll pay off in the long run as you build a growing base of loyal fans.

One thing to keep in mind is that on Facebook, if someone posts a message on your page, your reply will be nested under that post similar to a forum thread. In Twitter, there's no clear sequence of each conversation, and all of your Tweets are just displayed in reverse chronological order, both on your profile page and on your followers' feeds. Because of this, it's vital to include some context in each reply, or else you'll have a bunch of Tweets saying nothing but "thanks". Whereas this is fine on Facebook, it'll get annoying quickly on Twitter because all of your followers will receive all your Tweets on their feeds, whether directed at them or not.

So if someone sends you a Tweet saying "Dr. Smith is the best chiropractor in town! My back pain is completely gone", instead of just replying "Thanks for the compliment" or something to that effect, say "Thanks for the compliment! I'm glad your back is finally feeling better." This way, when your other followers read that Tweet, at least they'll have an idea of what you're talking about.

Another option is to send direct messages for all responses that don't pertain to your entire follower base. A direct message doesn't appear on feeds and can only be seen by the intended recipient.

If possible, always try to respond to any message you receive within a 24 hour period, besides weekends, holidays, etc. People of the Internet world tend to expect fast response times, especially if it's a customer service issue.

Occasionally, you'll receive vocal complaints about your business on these social media sites. Social media has basically given every person an outlet they can vent to. These complaints, legit or not, must be dealt with accordingly. The way to properly handle them will be discussed in chapter 7, since it's way more than just a social media issue.

6. Video SEO
"No Steven Spielbergs Allowed"

Video marketing is by far my favorite subject to talk about. Not only is it one of the most effective ways to market your local business, it's also one of the easiest. Of course, I am not saying that you should focus on video and nothing else, as the methods I'm covering in this book tend to work best when used together. However, video marketing is capable of generating results rapidly, usually within weeks. So while you're tackling SEO for your website (which as I said before typically takes 3-6 months before you'll see any results), you should definitely use video marketing to bring in leads in the meantime.

By the way, when I say video marketing in this book, what I really mean is YouTube marketing. While there are hundreds of video sharing sites on the Internet, YouTube videos get the lion's share of views. I focus on getting YouTube videos ranked alongside regular website listings on Google. After all, it'd be pretty pointless to simply rank high on Google Videos or YouTube. Who's going to search for a video when they're looking for a local business?

So let's say my windshield is broken and I search for "emergency windshield repair Houston" on Google. Here are the search results I get:

```
emergency windshield repair houston
```

About 372,000 results (0.22 seconds)

Ads related to emergency windshield repair houston   Why these ads?

281-614-9837 Call 24/7 - Water Removal-Disinfect-Drying
www.houstonrestoration.com/
Direct Ins. Billing A+ BBB Rating

Roofi Repair Specialist - A+ Rated With The BBB
www.advancedroofinghouston.com/
All Workmenship Is guaranteed.
   7941 Katy FreeWay, #155, Houston, TX
   (832) 593-4255 - Directions

Guaranteed Roof Repair | americanhoustonroofing.com
www.americanhoustonroofing.com/Roof
Same Day Service for Leak **Repairs** All Types Roof **Repairs** 281-690-6620

713-774-5277 Emergency Auto Glass Replacement Houston Texas
www.squidoo.com › ... › Car Maintenance › General Car Maintenance
Jun 30, 2012 – We offer **Emergency Auto Glass Replacement** in **Houston** Texas Did you just suffer from auto glass breakage? Have a big crack in you ...

Windshield Repair Houston | 713-893-5096 | Emergency - YouTube

www.youtube.com/watch?v=iU92ta408F0
Jul 10, 2012 - 2 min - Uploaded by WindshieldHouston
Windshield Repair Houston - 713-893-5096 - Call now for a free quote on windshield/**auto glass repair** or ...

More videos for emergency windshield repair houston »

Auto Glass Replacement Company - West Oaks - **Houston, TX**
www.yelp.com › Automotive › Auto Glass Services
Specialties: 281 496 2401 Written lifetime warranty on All Work **Emergency** mobile ... **Houston**,Hunters Creek Village,**windshield repair** and replacement expert ...

You can see down in the organic results that my video is ranking #2 (the top 3 results are pay-per-click ads). It generates a good number of calls and leads every month for my client.

You may have also noticed that the video stands out way more than the regular website listings surrounding it, simply because it has a thumbnail image attached to it.

Indeed, we humans are visual creatures by nature. Search engine results pages typically contain nothing but text, so when there is an image available on such a page, our eyes are drawn to it automatically.

This is one major reason why video marketing is so powerful. It allows you to stand out, and we all know how difficult that is to accomplish on the Internet.

You may be thinking that it's hard or expensive to make a video. This couldn't be further from the truth. Nearly all the videos on YouTube, including many of the viral ones with millions of views, were not shot professionally. They're mostly recorded by a simple webcam, smartphone, or cheap digital camera.

I understand that as a business owner, you always want to appear professional. However, this does not mean you have to hire a videographer who will charge you $500 or more for each 2-minute video created. In the past we have done tests where we'd upload both average homemade videos as well as professionally done videos for the same company. Guess what? Homemade videos produced better results! Consumers are just so tired of seeing advertisements on TV that they don't want any more of it online. And yes, professionally made videos for a local business often resemble regular TV advertisements a bit too much.

So what types of videos can you make? You have a ton of options, and on the follow pages, I've listed some of the best ones.

Record Yourself Giving Industry Related Tips on Video

These make the best marketing tools for you as a local business owner because they educate your prospective customers, position you as an authority in the field, and can include call to action.

Let's go back to our chiropractor example. There are a lot of health problems a chiropractor can help alleviate or eliminate, such as:

- Back pain
- Shoulder pain
- Neck pain
- Join pain
- Headaches
- Scoliosis
- Bulging disc
- Herniated disc
- Frozen shoulder
- Pain management
- Sports rehabilitation

I'm sure there are many more, but you get my point. As a chiropractor, it would not be hard at all to film a 1-2 minute video for each of these topics. For example, in the back pain video, the chiropractor can talk about what the typical causes for back pain are, offer a few tips on how to reduce back pain, and list some bad habits to avoid in order to prevent the pain from reoccurring. It really is as simple as that.

At the end of each video, you should throw in a

clear call to action. Something along the lines of "if you would like more information on how to eradicate your back pain once and for all, please call..." or "we can guide you onto the road of recovery, call us for a free consultation..."

Although each of these is basically just a self-pitch, it won't bother people at all because you've already provided value in the video. If they watched it until the end, chances are they are very interested in what you have to say. This is why you absolutely must steer them in the direction you want - be it to give you a call, visit your website, join your mailing list, or what have you. Just implementing this one technique can literally double your conversion rates.

Now even though you shouldn't spend an arm and leg hiring a professional videographer, you still must dress professionally while recording these videos. The best idea is to simply play the part of your profession. If you're a personal trainer, wear workout clothes. If you're a doctor, wear your white coat, and so on. In other words, dress the way you would when you are interacting with customers. This practice naturally instills more trust into viewers.

Here's an example of an educational video filmed for one of our clients:

http://getinternetexposure.com/video1

Notice how professional it looks even though it was recorded with an affordable digital camera.

Slideshow Videos of Your Business

If for some reason you can't or don't want to record videos of yourself talking, you can always produce simple slideshow videos. Keep in mind that they will not convert as well as educational videos because they typically offer less value to viewers.

To start, you'll need 10-15 pictures. This part is easy. Simply take some pictures of yourself, your office (both interior and exterior), and even your staff/customers if they don't mind (but make sure you get their consent in writing just in case). Even stock photos you can purchase on the Internet will work fine if all else fails.

And if you can, take pictures of your portfolio or results of work you've done. This option is obviously not available for all businesses, but for industries like custom painting, home remodeling, or pool building, it works wonderfully. Remember, your ability to impart relevant information in a slideshow video is almost nil, since you won't be talking and nobody really wants to read a bunch of text while watching a video. So your next best bet is to show off your work.

For service industries where there are no real tangible results to show, you'll have to be creative and tell a "story" in your video. Let's take AC repair for example. A broken AC is not going to look any different from a working one, at least not to a typical consumer who has no knowledge of how an AC works internally. In this case, here's how you can use a sequence of images and text to tell a story:

1. Identify the problem (text): "Did your AC break down? Is it unbearably HOT inside your home?"

2. Show a few pictures of unhappy people fanning themselves in the hot weather, a photo of a thermostat displaying 90 degrees, etc.

3. Offer a solution (text): "For emergency AC repair now - Call..."

4. Show pictures of you and your staff, preferably on a jobsite repairing an AC unit. Pictures of your company vehicle(s) and equipment will work as well.

5. Instill positive expectation (text): "Get your AC working again as early as tonight!"

6. Show pictures of happy families, including kids and pets. You can use stock photos or photos of your actual customers, if they give you permission.

7. Call to action (text): "Don't wait, call now! Bob's AC Repair - (xxx) xxx-xxxx"

Basically, I'm telling my prospective customers that if they call, their AC will be up and running again in no time, and they won't have to suffer in the heat anymore. Although I didn't provide much useful information, I'm offering them a solution to a major problem, which is in itself valuable.

Notice that the video never mentions the words "I", "we", "me", "us", etc. It's all about **you** (directed at the prospective customer) - "is **your** AC broken", "is **your** home hot", "get **your** AC working again", etc. This is important because people don't care about you. They want to know how you can solve their problem and that's it.

There are many other topics you can make slideshow videos about as well. Below are some ideas to get you started:

- Before and after photos of your past work - this is great for hair stylists, home remodelers, maids, etc.

- Showcase products and services you offer.
- Offer coupons or promotional deals. Either create some for the video or use your existing ones.
- Provided that your online reviews are good, take screenshots of your high ratings from around the web and compile them into a video. Then you can title your video something like "Dr. John Smith - Rated Best Chiropractor in Houston". Believe me, consumers care a great deal about online reviews. I'll be going into much more detail on this topic in the next chapter.
- Basic information about your business - name, services offered, phone number, driving directions, etc. Since this type of video tends to be text-oriented, be sure to mix in pictures and perhaps a map.

Remember to always try and keep the text to a minimum. Each text slide should not exceed 15 words. You have to give people enough time to read all that text before the video moves on to the next slide.

Creating a slideshow video is extremely simple and can be accomplished by using free software like Windows Movie Maker. However, if you want to create more professional videos, consider signing up for a service like Animoto (http://animoto.com) or Proshow Web (http://www.photodex.com/proshow/web). Creating a video on either of these platforms is as simple as selecting a theme, uploading photos, and adding text/soundtrack if desired. Sleek effects and transitions are then added in automatically to spice up your video.

Here's an example of a "before and after" slideshow video created for a local hair stylist:

http://getinternetexposure.com/video2

Video Scribing (Also Known As Whiteboard Animation)

This is a relatively new method to create professional, attention-grabbing videos. Basically, each video goes through the motions of drawing a variety of objects and writing short lines of text, telling a story in the process. This is a bit difficult to explain in words, so check out the website below and play the video on the page for some examples:

http://getinternetexposure.com/videoscribe

As you can see, these videos are super sleek. That's why companies often charge thousands of dollars to create them. Luckily, with the right software, this type of video is incredibly easy to make. VideoScribe by Sparkol (linked above) is the program I use. At the time of this writing, it only costs about $20 per month for a pro account, which allows for unlimited video production and full commercial usage.

The software includes a large library of clipart you can use. Whatever idea you want to present, you will more than likely be able to find a clipart that fits perfectly. Let's go back and remake the slideshow video for our fictitious AC repair company using VideoScribe:

1. Identify the problem (text): "Did your AC break down? Is it unbearably HOT inside your home?"

2. Draw a bright sun. Then draw a frustrated or angry person or two right below the sun. Ideally you'll want a picture of a sweating person, but that might not be available because it's too specific. As you create these videos, you'll find that even generic pictures work great as long as you clearly define the context.

3. Offer a solution (text): "For emergency AC

repair now - Call..."

4. Draw a few pictures related to air conditioning, such as an AC unit, a repairman or handyman (because again, "AC repairman" is far too specific and you probably won't find a clipart of one), a toolbox, and so on.

5. Instill positive expectation (text): "Get your AC working again as early as tonight!"

6. Draw pictures of happy people, including kids and pets. If you can find a clipart of a functional AC or even a fan blowing, that would be a nice addition.

7. Call to action (text): "Don't wait, call now! Bob's AC Repair - (xxx) xxx-xxxx"

Even though the basic storyline is virtually identical to our slideshow video, the presentation is extremely different. Your result is a unique, fun, and possibly quirky video that will instantly catch the viewer's attention.

You can also choose to add voiceover if you'd like. Keep in mind that it's a tricky endeavor, because you have to match your spoken words to what's being drawn or written on the video. In other words, you'll probably have to alter the speed at which you speak. The Sparkol software does allow you to record a voiceover, and I highly recommend that you do. Your viewers would rather listen to you talk than read a bunch of text.

Also, don't discount the effectiveness of such videos just because they are animated. They are still extremely professional, and I'm sure the word "childish" never came to mind when you watched the samples above. People appreciate something fresh and new, and very few businesses utilize this particular type of video in their marketing strategy at the moment.

As you can probably tell, video scribing requires more creativity than the other methods we discussed, and the video creation process itself has a steeper learning curve. Is it worth it? Absolutely, if for no other reason than the fact that it allows you to stand out among your competitors.

You can use any or all of these methods to create simple but effective videos. And if you would like to, you can go one step further and add background music to your videos. I especially recommend this for videos without any voiceovers since they will otherwise have no sound at all, which is pretty bland and not very engaging to viewers.

If you are using Proshow Web, Animoto, or Sparkol, each of these programs already includes a library of royalty free music you can choose from. There are also many websites where you can purchase royalty free music. My favorite one is http://www.jewelbeat.com - every song here is only $0.99.

Important! Be sure to only use royalty free music! If you don't stick to this rule and YouTube finds out that you're using copyrighted music, the video in question or even your entire account may be deleted. Worse yet, the artist could decide to sue you. Granted, this doesn't happen very often, but it's still wise to take precautions.

Ranking Your Videos

Now that you have your videos created, it's time to upload and rank them.

First, you need to create a YouTube account for your business. You should select a YouTube username that incorporates your industry and location. So if you are a chiropractor in Katy, TX, your ideal username would be "KatyChiropractor" or "ChiropractorKaty". This tells both your human viewers and search engines what your channel is about. If you choose an arbitrary username like "JGrant4778", your YouTube channel could be about anything and you cannot position yourself as an authority in the chiropractic (or any) niche.

It's very likely that your desired username is either taken already or too long to fit within YouTube's username guidelines. In this case you'll have to be a little creative. Add numbers, add your state after the city, use abbreviations for longer words, change the order of the words, and so on.

For example, if I own a limousine rental company in Houston, TX, I'll want the username "LimousineRentalHouston", which is too long (YouTube only allows up to 20 characters for usernames). I'll instead use "LimoRentalHouston". If that's taken, I can always try "HoustonLimoRental" or "LimoRentalHoustonTX". And if all else fails, I'll add a number or two at the end.

The most important thing to keep in mind here is that you always want to get a username that's as relevant to your industry and location as possible, even if it's not the exact keyword you want. Numbers in your channel name are not aesthetically pleasing to look at, but will not affect your search engine rankings. Still, avoid using them when you can, and use as few as possible when there's no other choice.

This might be obvious, but once you have your YouTube channel created, only upload business-related videos to it. Don't upload videos of your dog, child, or anything else onto the same channel. Create a second YouTube account for your personal videos.

After you upload each video, you'll need to fill out its title, description, and tags. Let's go over each component in detail.

Title

Your video's title is by far the most important piece of information for ranking in search engines as well as generating clicks and leads. You are allowed up to 100 characters in the title, and I suggest that you make full use of them. Here's the title of a video I created for a local chiropractor:

Back Pain Relief | 281-xxx-xxxx | Katy TX 77494 | Hip Pain | Shoulder Pain | Natural Painkiller

It's 95 characters long, and I used pipes (the "|" - which is shift-backslash) to separate my keywords. Some video marketers prefer to use dashes instead, but I think pipes are more aesthetically pleasing, and YouTube seems to recognize them as "idea separators."

The main keyword you are targeting in your video must be listed first in the title. For my example video, it's "back pain relief." I've added the phone number next, because believe it or not, some prospective customers will not even bother to watch the video at all. They simply pick up the phone and call the number listed.

For my third block of text, I've listed the city, state, and zip code I'm targeting. This part is pretty self-explanatory. Geo-targeting is crucial for local businesses because they operate within limited service areas. A chiropractor in Katy, TX cannot help someone who lives in Washington D.C.

The next 3 sets are all additional keywords I'm targeting. Because the video I made is a fairly generic one about pain management, I can add in other pain related keywords. But even if your video is pretty specific, you will always be able to find related keywords if you look and think hard enough. Make each title as close to 100 characters (without going over, of course) as you can.

Description

First and foremost, your video's description must start with the main keyword you're targeting, as well as a clear call to action. For my chiropractor video, I wrote:

Back pain relief fast - Call xxx-xxx-xxxx now for Dr. Smith, your local Katy chiropractor.

On the second or third line (depending on how long your first sentence is), you should add your website URL. Some viewers may want to check out your website before picking up the phone.

As a side note, only the first 3 lines of a video description are visible to the viewer unless he clicks "Show More". Most people won't, which is why you should always include the most vital information up at the top.

Your description should not just end here, however. Even though most viewers will not be reading the rest, Google will. There is a lot of anecdotal evidence suggesting that longer descriptions are favored over shorter ones as far as Google rankings go. You can have up to 5,000 characters in your description, and while you certainly don't have to use them all, you should strive to provide as much relevant content as you can.

Here are some ideas on what you can include in your description:

- Your business address and a link to your Google local listing
- A list of services you offer
- Your service area (list specific neighborhoods, towns, and zip codes)
- Your hours of operation
- Current discount coupons and special deals
- Industry information and tips for the consumer (you can even copy content from your website)

Tags

Tags are not very important. Just list the main keyword you're targeting as well as a few other related keywords. For my chiropractor video, I used all the keywords in my title in conjunction with my location. So my tags are "back pain relief Katy", "hip pain Katy", "shoulder pain Katy", and "natural painkiller Katy".

If at all possible, be sure to create a sense of urgency in your videos. For example, pain is naturally an urgent matter. When someone is experiencing pain, their main priority is to get rid of it as soon as possible. Therefore, a prospective customer who's currently in pain is a lot more likely to pick up the phone and call for the earliest available appointment without any hesitation. They are less likely to ask for discounts or shop around for the best prices.

Add urgent keywords such as "emergency", "fast", "quick", "today", "24 hour", and "same day" to your video titles. I realize that this won't be applicable to all niches, but you can always find your prospective customers' pain points. Even if you offer a service that's not typically top priority for most people, such as dry cleaning, you can still instill urgency. A customer may have a wedding coming up that he forgot about, or has to give a presentation on short notice. In both of these scenarios, fast dry cleaning service becomes a necessity and you can position your pitch in a way that caters to this demographic.

Of course, the premise here is that your company actually does offer emergency services. Don't use these keywords if you can't deliver.

Video Sets

Because there are tons of keywords I can target for each industry, I will typically create anywhere between 5 and 50 videos for a business in order to gain maximum exposure. This is an important concept, because unlike websites, videos are much easier and less time consuming to make. You'd be leaving money on the table if you didn't try to cover as much ground as possible with video marketing.

For my Katy chiropractor campaign, I created a total of 14 videos with the following titles:

VIDEO SEO - NO STEVEN SPIELBERGS ALLOWED

- Carpal Tunnel | 281-xxx-xxxx | Katy TX 77449 | Ankle Pain Relief | Joint Pain Relief | Chiropractor
- Shoulder Pain | 281-xxx-xxxx | Katy Texas 77450 | Spinal Stenosis | Neck Pain Relief | Emergency
- Low Back Pain | 281-xxx-xxxx | Katy TX 77494 | Tennis Elbow | Treatment for TMJ | Immediate Relief
- Neck Pain | 281-xxx-xxxx | Katy TX 77493 | Whiplash | Spinal Decompression | Fast Pain Relief Now
- Sciatica | 281-xxx-xxxx | Katy Texas 77493 | Pinched Nerve | Shoulder and Neck Pain Relief | Urgent
- Knee Pain Relief | 281-xxx-xxxx | Katy Texas 77494 | Knee Injury | Chiropractic Clinic | Hand Pain
- Lower Back Pain | 281-xxx-xxxx | Katy TX 77450 | Car Accident Injury | Joint Pains | Pain Relief
- Fibromyalgia Treatment | 281-xxx-xxxx | Katy TX 77449 | Back Ache | Frozen Shoulder | Chiropractic
- Leg Pain Relief | 281-xxx-xxxx | Katy TX 77449 | Back Pains | Sports Injuries | Foot Pain Relief
- Headaches | 281-xxx-xxxx | Katy Texas 77450 | Herniated Disc | Elbow Pain Relief | Katy Chiropractor
- Back Pain Relief | 281-xxx-xxxx | Katy TX 77494 | Hip Pain | Shoulder Pain | Natural Painkiller
- Chiropractic Care | 281-xxx-xxxx | Katy Texas 77493 | Acupuncture | Neck Pain Relief | Wrist Pain
- Chiropractor in Katy | 281-xxx-xxxx | 77450 | Joint Pain | Bulging Disc | Sore Muscles | Quick
- Katy Chiropractor | 281-xxx-xxxx | Chiropractor Katy | Fast Pain Relief | 77494 | Free Consultation

Each video title contains 3-4 keywords, as well as the business's phone number and location information. Even though Katy is a small suburban town, it still encompasses 4 zip codes. I basically alternated between them in my titles. I also use "TX" and "Texas" interchangeably, since people will conduct searches using both variations.

With a set up like this, my videos can be found on page one across over a hundred keywords. Even if each keyword only gets 10 searches per month, that's over a thousand pair of eyes on my videos every month.

You see, most of these keywords aren't going to get a lot of searches, especially not in a local context (for instance, the keyword "joint pain" by itself gets tons of searches, but "joint pain Katy" doesn't). By extension this means that the competition level for these keywords is going to be much lower, and you'll be able to rank for them easier.

Unless you're trying to target a large metropolitan area, your videos will rank and start generating leads without any additional SEO work, provided that you've properly optimized them by following the guidelines described earlier.

But what if your business just happens to be located in a large city that's super competitive? Houston is a prime example. Pick any type of business and you'll find hundreds, if not thousands of them. You'd be up against at least a few dozen companies who have professional SEO teams working to rank them for the top industry terms. You may be able to hit page one for a few long tail keywords (which are phrases with 3 or more words that are often very specific and have low search volume), but that's about it.

The key here is to create videos targeting small towns/suburbs/villages within the metropolitan area. Each large city has many of these. Houston has more than 100, Katy being one of them.

If your business has a relatively small service area

(i.e. auto repair shop - consumers will rarely drive more than 5 miles to get their cars fixed), then this will be easy. Target the town you're in as well as a few surrounding ones. Don't forget to rotate the zip codes in the video titles for each area.

If, on the other hand, you service the entire metropolitan area (i.e. AC contractors and custom pool builders), you have a lot more work to do. If you were to make a set of 14 videos for each town within Houston, you'd have to create over 1400 videos. But you don't have to create all of them at once. I recommend that you start slow and make video marketing a part of your long term promotional strategy. Target areas closest to you first, and then branch out from there. The number of leads you receive will increase over time.

Don't stress over the sheer number of videos that must be created. Once you get the hang of it, you'll find that it doesn't take much time. The initial keyword research stage is the toughest, but once you finish the first set of video titles, they can be reused with few changes for other towns/suburbs you want to target (namely, only the city and zip code must be changed).

The videos themselves don't have to be too different from each other either. Yes, they all must be unique, because YouTube does not allow duplicate content, but videos with minor differences are still considered unique. Some tweaks you can make include adding or subtracting a few images, and changing the background music.

Keep in mind that you should still create videos for the major metropolitan area **in addition** to ones that target small towns. Because of the higher search volume, you'll pick up quite a few leads even if your videos don't rank that well.

Speaking of which, videos targeting the top keyword for each industry will almost never rank on the first page on their own, even in small towns. For instance, every chiropractor in Katy is gunning after the keyword "Katy chiropractor", and there are over 100 chiropractors actively practicing in Katy. Now imagine how many chiropractors there are in a large city like Houston, and what the competition level might be like.

Of course, it's not impossible to rank your video on the first page for these competitive search terms. However, you'll have to do some extensive off-site SEO work. The strategies I laid out in the website SEO section (chapter 2) work remarkably well for videos as well. But again, don't be dejected if you don't see any results within a month or two. Even though videos are often easier to rank than websites, it can still take a very long time.

Final Notes

You should focus on uploading videos to YouTube and ranking them on Google. Google owns YouTube, and most Internet marketers speculate that this is why it takes less effort and time to rank a YouTube video than a regular website. It makes sense that Google would prefer their own properties over everything else.

That being said, if you're completely done with your YouTube campaign, there's no reason not to upload your videos to the many other video sharing websites available. After all, more exposure is always a good thing. Here are a few other popular video sharing sites you can upload to:

- http://www.metacafe.com

- http://www.dailymotion.com
- http://www.vimeo.com
- http://www.veoh.com
- http://www.blip.tv
- http://www.photobucket.com

Keep in mind that each site has different terms and possibly different character limits for video titles, descriptions, and tags.

Another important detail to note is that at this point in time, search engines other than Google, including Yahoo and Bing, are not very video-friendly, and you shouldn't worry about trying to rank your videos in them (yet). Nevertheless, the fact that over 65% of all search queries are conducted on Google makes video marketing an already extremely profitable endeavor.

7. Reputation Management
"BBB of the Web"

Let's now put ourselves in a typical consumer's shoes, and this hypothetical consumer is looking for a pizza restaurant in Katy, TX (a suburb of Houston). He has typed "pizza in katy tx" into Google and found these results:

Fuzzy's **Pizza**
www.fuzzyspizzakaty.com/
Score: **16** / 30 - 23 Google reviews

(A) 613 South Mason Road
Katy
(281) 579-0100

Mazzei's Gourmet **Pizza**
mazzeisgourmetpizza.com/
Score: **28** / 30 - 25 Google reviews

(B) 6868 South Mason Road
Katy
(281) 579-1677

Pizza Bella
www.pizzabellakaty.com/
Score: **23** / 30 - 10 Google reviews

(C) 1306 Pin Oak Road
Katy
(281) 693-3880

New York Pizzeria
www.nypizzeria.com/
Score: **14** / 30 - 20 Google reviews

(D) 24210 Westheimer
Parkway
Katy
(281) 392-5323

Candelari's Pizzeria
www.candelaris.com/
Zagat: **16** / 30 - 26 Google reviews

(E) 6825 South Fry Road
Katy
(281) 395-6746

Palios **Pizza** Cafe
www.paliospizza.us/
9 Google reviews

(F) Suite K. 1450 W Grand
Pkwy S
Katy
(281) 392-1212

Buck's **Pizza**
www.buckspizza.com/
Google+ page

(G) 2944 South Mason Road
Katy
(281) 392-8257

More results near **Katy, TX** »

As you can see, the top 7 results are all Google Local listings. Each one of the top 5 listings has a posted score out of 30 points. This is the new Zagat rating system that Google recently adopted. If you're unfamiliar with it, here's the breakdown:

26-30   Extraordinary to perfection
21-25   Very good to excellent
16-20   Good to very good
11-15   Fair to good
0-10   Poor to fair

For a more detailed explanation of Google's ranking system, visit

http://getinternetexposure.com/zagat

Each business needs a minimum of 10 reviews before it will get an average score, which is why listings #6 and 7 (Palios Pizza Cafe and Buck's Pizza) do not have scores listed.

Right off the bat you can see that Mazzei's Gourmet Pizza (#2) has a score of 28 out of 30, by far the highest of the bunch. For most consumers, their search is now over. Remember, people are always busy and on the go. The faster they can make a decision, the better. Even if they do decide to read a couple of reviews here and there, chances are good that they'll come to the same decision at the end.

Which pizza restaurant would you choose? If you hold no existing bias, I'd be surprised if you choose one other than Mazzei's.

Of course, industry matters a ton. For a pizza restaurant the price to pay for a poor decision isn't nearly as great as choosing a dishonest car dealer. The higher a product or service costs, the more research a consumer will do.

It's worth noting that even though Fuzzy's Pizza is #1 on the list, it probably receives fewer clicks than Mazzei's. If these were regular organic website listings, Fuzzy's would get far more clicks, no doubt about it. In this case, the posted scores change everything.

So as you can see, gathering reviews from your current and past customers is extremely important, especially since 72% of all consumers trust online reviews just as much as personal recommendations from friends and family (i.e. word of mouth) according to a survey conducted by Search Engine Land in 2011. To read the full results of this study, please visit:

http://getinternetexposure.com/onlinereviews

Remember how I mentioned earlier that most business owners believe word of mouth to be the #1 advertising method? That's slowly changing. If you're ranked high on review sites, it's far more likely for a potential customer to be reading your online reviews than receiving a personal recommendation about your business.

Also, the same survey was conducted back in 2010 as well, and at that time 67% of all consumers said they trust online reviews just as much as personal recommendations. So this number has increased significantly in only a year, and in all likelihood will continue to rise over time.

What does this mean for you as a local business owner?

The answer is simple - collectively, positive online reviews make a fantastic lead generation tool for you.

Gathering Reviews

We all know that getting positive reviews is not an easy task. Typically, good service is expected and not rewarded, while unhappy customers are much more likely to take the time to post negative reviews.

This creates a dilemma for many local business owners, because online reviews usually over represent unsatisfied customers, unless you have a reputation management program in place.

You can certainly provide customers incentives to leave reviews, but you must be very careful. Avoid giving out cash rewards, and never require a positive review. It's perfectly okay to offer a discount coupon in exchange for a review, but you must do so for all reviews - positive or negative. Otherwise your actions could be considered bribery and you may be breaking FTC laws. Consult a legal professional if you are in doubt.

Whether you offer incentives or not, it's wise to set up a "review station" inside your business. This can be a computer, laptop or even iPad. Keep your Google local listing (or any other listing you want reviews on) open in a browser window so people can easily log in to post the review.

There are many review sites on the Internet, but the 5 most important ones are:

- Google Local - http://www.google.com/places/
- Yahoo Local - http://local.yahoo.com/
- Bing Local - http://www.bing.com/local/
- Yelp - http://www.yelp.com/
- CitySearch - http://www.citysearch.com/

The first 3 are important because together, they handle over 90% of all search queries on the Internet, many of them being local searches. Yelp and CitySearch, on the other hand, are two of the most well known local business directories.

You'll want reviews on all of these sites. You don't need to rush. Just take it one step at a time. Keep your Google Local listing on for a few months until you have 10 or 15 reviews, then move onto the next one. If you want steady growth on all sites at once, you can always gather Google reviews on Mondays, Yahoo reviews on Tuesdays, Bing reviews on Wednesdays, and so on. I do suggest that you work on Google first because it's where you'll get the most leads.

Don't forget to casually ask customers (while they're checking out or waiting) if they will spare a few minutes to leave you a review. If you offer incentives, have your customers show you the review they left in exchange for the reward. Even though you cannot explicitly tell them to leave positive reviews, in my experience no one will show you a negative review and ask for the reward without at least trying to resolve the problem with you first.

Negative Reviews

No matter how well you treat your customers and how great your products/services are, there will always be difficult customers who leave you bad reviews. Depending on your industry, even one negative review can be detrimental to your business, especially since consumers are relying on online reviews more and more.

For restaurants, an occasional negative review isn't

a big deal. Service levels in restaurants tend to fluctuate depending on how busy the wait staff is, whether there are new employees in training, which chef is working, etc. People know and expect this. (Note: if **most** or **all** reviews for a restaurant are bad, that's a huge red flag.) On the other hand, if there is a single detailed negative review on the front page of a custom pool builder's listing, it alone can steer away many potential customers. The sheer high dollar value of a new pool forces most people to be extremely conservative when choosing a company to work with.

If a customer does leave a bad review for you online, the rule of thumb is to always respond in a professional manner as soon as possible. Depending on the situation, you may want to simply apologize and ask if there's anything you can do. Or, if you've already done everything in your power to make that customer happy, here's your chance to explain your side of the story. Just remember to stay courteous no matter what kind of attitude the customer exhibits.

By consistently responding to negative reviews, you are showing prospective customers that you really care, and you're not some faceless corporation who pays no attention to what people are saying. There is also a chance that you will work something out with an unhappy customer and turn him/her into a happy one.

However, sometimes simply responding to negative reviews is not enough, and they will continue to affect your business. Unfortunately there is no reliable way to remove negative reviews, despite what anyone else may tell you. Every local site gives you a way to report inappropriate reviews, but in most cases the sites will choose not to remove them. Remember, these sites want to retain the integrity of their systems. So if they deem a review to be legitimate (even if in reality it's not), it will stay on the site.

Google, for instance, has been known to only remove reviews that are completely irrelevant (spam) or contain illegal content/foul language. If the negative review in question does not fall into one of these categories, you pretty much have no case. Even if Google does decide to remove a review, it can take them weeks or even months to actually do so.

The best way to lessen the effect of a negative review is to keep getting new, positive reviews on your listing, which will appear above the one you don't want anyone to see. Eventually, that negative one will be buried on page 2, and people rarely read past the first page of reviews.

Again, let me reiterate that no matter how customer-centric your business is, you will still get negative reviews. You definitely can and should do your best to please all of your customers, but don't lose sleep over one negative review. Focus on gathering more positive ones to displace the bad apple.

Social Media

When someone leaves you a negative review on Google, Yelp, etc., they're typically not trying to work it out with you and are just looking to vent/share their bad experience with others (although there are always exceptions). If someone complains to you on Facebook or Twitter, they very likely **are** expecting a response and possibly compensation if they feel they've been wronged.

So reply to the dissatisfied customer as soon as

possible, listen to his or her side of the story, and work hard to resolve the issue at hand. If you're successful and that customer turns into a happy one, you've not only prevented him from posting negative reviews on your local listings, but your other Facebook fans or Twitter followers will witness the way you handled that situation and commend you for it.

Remember, social media users are often very vocal on the Internet. You can bet that they'll write negative reviews about you on every site they can find you on if you make the mistake of ignoring them.

Additional Tips

- People who write positive reviews for you on local listing sites do not typically expect a response, but you should still respond to them from time to time. Thank your customers for taking the time to post a review for you.
- As demonstrated by our pizza restaurant example, ranking first on Google is not as important as making your business stand out among your competitors. This could mean having better and more reviews than them. For instance, if you are ranked #3, but #1 only has a 13/30 rating and #2 has no reviews at all, you will still get more clicks than both of them if you have a 25/30 rating or higher with a good number of total customer reviews.
- In addition to a review station, you can take it one step further and also keep a testimonial book. A testimonial book is a simply a binder filled with written customer testimonials. But each page can include far more than just a testimonial; it can ask detailed questions such as

how the customer rates your business in terms of service quality and speed, staff friendliness, etc. It can also ask the customer for suggestions on how you can improve your service. All in all, it's more like a customer satisfaction survey.

Repeat customers are ideal respondents for your testimonial book, because it takes more time to complete than just a simple review. You can also use the data gathered for market research purposes and gain valuable insight on how your customers feel about you.

You may be thinking to yourself that this all sounds like a huge, frustrating time sink, and you're right. Reputation management is one of the most dreaded components of owning a local business, right up there with doing taxes. That's why many local businesses opt to hire a reputation management firm. They will basically take over the management of your review sites, monitor incoming reviews and respond promptly. Most of them will also post new positive reviews for you.

If you're considering going this route, please be aware of false promises. Again, there is no surefire way to remove negative reviews from your local listings, save for deleting the entire page and starting over completely. And this might be the way to go in extreme cases where you think a particular listing is so overwhelmed with negative reviews that it can't be salvaged. But if you have mostly positive reviews and you want the few bad apples removed, don't count on it. Some firms will claim that they can do this for you, and by this they mean they will go and report the reviews as inappropriate, hoping that the review site will do something about it.

The problem is that the review sites still get the final say on whether they will remove a review or not. And in the vast majority of cases, they will not. Reputation management companies have absolutely no control over this, although they may try to convince you otherwise.

Another important point to consider is ethics. Many companies will use dishonest means to increase your ratings, such as by adding fake positive reviews for you or even posting negative reviews on your competitors' listings to make you look better. Is that really what you want?

I'm a firm believer in doing things the honest way. And yes, there are ethical ways you can approach reputation management.

For example, in my marketing company (we do take on reputation management clients), we understand how difficult it can be to gather positive reviews, even with a review station properly set up. There's a myriad of reasons for this, including:

- People don't already have an account to post a review with and don't want to sign up on the spot. Yes, most people will have Google accounts, but when you're collecting reviews for your CitySearch or Bing listings, you'll find that very few have these less popular accounts.
- People don't want to log into their accounts on a public computer for privacy reasons.
- Technical difficulties - maybe the computer crashed, or a previous customer accidentally closed the review site, maybe some customers aren't familiar with the review site and don't know how to actually leave a review, etc. The list goes on and on. This is particularly true in industries where most customers are older.

To bypass these issues, we design review cards for each business we work with that can be handed out to customers. Most customers will have no problem with handwriting a short review if they are happy with the product or service. We then take these positive reviews and post them onto our client's local listings slowly but consistently. Typically, adding one or two new reviews per week is a good pace for most businesses, depending on how fast they were getting reviews before.

Here's a sample review card we created for a salon:

If you hire a firm to do this, make sure that they do not post too many reviews too fast. If your business received 5 reviews total last year, it would be extremely suspicious, both to Google and prospective customers, if you suddenly start getting 10 reviews per day, even if they are valid and real. Also, it's wise to consider how many reviews your competitors have. If they each have less than 5, and you alone have over 100, that could raise a red flag as well.

As an added bonus, if the customer handwrites you a negative review, you can try to resolve the issue right then and there, *before* he gets the chance to leave. Because if he leaves an unhappy customer, he is a lot more likely to post negative reviews for you online when he gets home.

Also, please do not make the mistake of posting any reviews online yourself, even if they are real. The computer and account you are using are being tracked by review sites constantly. If multiple reviews to your business somehow get linked together, they may be considered fraudulent and get removed. In fact, your entire listing could be deleted if the offense is serious enough. Reputation management firms will make sure that the reviews being posted cannot be linked together under any circumstances.

As a reminder, be sure to keep all review cards on file. They are your proof in case anyone ever questions if your reviews are real, and they can become useful marketing materials later down the road.

In the end, it's up to you how you want to approach the reputation management beast. My suggestion is that you take it slow and go the ethical route. But whatever you decide, the single most important takeaway is this - reputation management is far too important to just be ignored.

8. Other Important Internet Marketing Concepts

I. Pay-Per-Click Advertising

I have not written much about pay-per-click ads (also known as PPC) previously in this book because honestly, it's probably not the best use of your time or money. For one thing, it's gotten so overly competitive in recent years that you'd be lucky to just break even in many local niches. In fact, certain keywords related to lawyers in Los Angeles are now costing advertisers over $50 a click.

You might think that these lawyers must still be making money, despite paying $50 a click, or they would stop running these ads. However, many PPC advertisers do not have an accurate way to track whether those clicks are actually generating leads and sales or not. Or, they may be able to assess that their PPC campaigns have increased their overall profit, but they're targeting 100 keywords and have no clue which ones are working and which aren't.

Because the vast majority of PPC campaigns are under optimized, advertisers are collectively paying more for ad clicks than they should, which in turn drives prices up. A new advertiser can lose large amounts of money very quickly if he's not careful. For this reason, I suggest starting on the low end when deciding how much you want to pay for each click, and run it for a week or two to see how many clicks you can realistically expect each day. Then increase it slowly from there until you hit the ideal level.

Also, PPC comes with an extremely steep learning curve (indeed, hundreds of books have been written on the topic). While the basic premise is easy, it will take a lot of time and money to truly master PPC. You'll need to monitor your campaigns on a daily basis, as the number of competing ads and conversion rates will vary over time.

That being said, PPC advertising does have its advantages. For one thing, it is hands down the fastest way to get customers in the door. You can put up an ad today and make a sale tomorrow. No other Internet marketing strategy can match this speed. Also, you only pay when someone actually clicks on your ad (thereby already showing interest in what you have to offer).

But before you create your first pay-per-click campaign, let's take a look at the two different types of PPC ads you can run:

PPC in search engines

These are the ads you see on Google, Yahoo, Bing, etc. when you do a search. They typically appear above and to the right of organic results. This type of PPC advertising is also known as search marketing.

When you run an ad of this sort, you'll be asked to select keywords you want to target and set the maximum

Pay-Per-Click Advertising

you're willing to pay per click. Once approved, your ad will start appearing on the search results pages of your chosen keywords.

Your ad's actual rank (typically only 10 ads are displayed per page) depends on several factors:

- Your maximum cost per click - the more you're willing to pay, the higher you'll rank.
- Content on your landing page (the webpage your ad links to) - the more relevant your landing page is to your ad and the keyword you're targeting, the higher you'll rank.
- Your PPC account status - ads created by a new account suffer a slight penalty in the rankings until that account becomes more established.

Like regular websites, there are also various hidden metrics search engines use to determine rankings for PPC ads. It's possible that your ad won't show up at all if its "score" (assigned by search engines based on a combination of your cost per click, landing page relevance, account status, and hidden metrics) is too low. In this case, you'll need to increase your bid, improve your landing page, or both.

The top search marketing platforms are:

- **Google Adwords** - https://adwords.google.com - extremely competitive and expensive, but can generate a very large amount of traffic to your website if you have the budget for it.
- **Bing Ads** - http://advertise.bingads.microsoft.com - now serves ads on both MSN/Bing and Yahoo. Advertising here won't generate as much traffic as running an ad on Google, but clicks cost significantly

less (roughly 50% less in most niches).

PPC in social networks

These are ads found on sites like Facebook and LinkedIn while you're logged in and browsing around. You will not be targeting keywords in this case, but rather specific subsets of demographics. Below are some targeting options on Facebook for your intended audience:

- Location
- Age
- Gender
- Likes and interests
- Relationship status
- Education level
- Workplace

For example, if you're selling high end bridal products, you can choose to target women who are engaged with an income of at least $50,000 per year. If you own a weight lifting gym, you might target men between the ages of 20 and 35 with "bodybuilding" selected as an interest. In both cases you can display your ad only to people who reside in your city or town.

The top social network PPC platforms are:

- **Facebook** - https://www.facebook.com/advertising - currently the world's largest social network. Unlike search engine PPC, Facebook allows you to include a 100 x 72 pixel image with every ad.
- **LinkedIn** - http://www.linkedin.com/advertising - geared towards business-to-business companies and companies serving working professionals. Currently, it's very expensive ($2.00 per click minimum).

Most of the time, search marketing is a better choice for local businesses than social network PPC. Being able to target specific keywords is more powerful because you can cater your ad and landing page to exactly what that searcher is looking for. So if your target keyword is "back pain relief Katy," you can use an ad like this:

> Suffering from Back Pain?
> Get rid of back pain for good!
> Visit us for a free consultation.
> KatyTXChiropractor.com

Your destination URL should lead to a subpage of your website that talks primarily about back pain. Provide informative, relevant content, such as home remedies for back pain and perhaps some recommended exercises. Include a strong call-to-action and offer an incentive for the visitor to book an appointment, sign up for your mailing list, like your Facebook fan page, etc. An example of a good incentive in this case would be a free or cheap initial consultation, or a discount on an adjustment.

But I'm sure you can already see the problem here. If you're targeting 50 keywords, you'd in turn have to create 50 different ad variations and 50 subpages on your website, all with unique content. It's simply not feasible for a typical local business owner to keep up with such a huge amount of work.

Luckily, there are scripts that will automatically change your ad and even designated words on your webpage based on what the search query is. Using such a script will automate a lot of the work required, as long as the keywords you target are mostly related. So for our chiropractor example, there are many different types of pain we could target, and the script can alter the ad to match the type of pain being searched for. For instance, if someone typed in "joint pain relief Katy", our ad would say "Suffering from Joint Pain? Get rid of your joint pain for good! Visit us for a free consultation." It would no longer mention back pain at all.

Be aware that if you go this route, your landing page can no longer be specifically about back pain. You'll have to create content that's generic enough to suit all of the keywords you're targeting. Of course, this task will be a breeze compared to creating 50 unique pages.

II. *Groupon, LivingSocial, etc.*

First off, I'm not here to bash Groupon or other similar sites. As a **consumer** I love Groupon. I can get awesome deals to establishments I already frequent, as well as try out new restaurants and fun activities at steep discounts. What's not to like?

But I'm someone you would consider a "coupon clipper." The desire to save money is deeply ingrained within my psyche. I can honestly say that I'm not your ideal customer. Because I've been so spoiled by Groupon, I never want to pay full price for anything. I'm always looking for more discounts, more savings, and I'm likely to ditch your business for the one right down the street if they can give me a better price (as long as their online ratings are comparable to yours).

This is how all coupon clippers think. And the vast majority of Groupon buyers fit snugly into this category. So, think about what kind of customers you're attracting with Groupon.

I'm not saying that you as a business owner cannot profit from Groupon. Many local businesses successfully use Groupon as a part of their marketing strategy. But you must be very careful and take the necessary steps to evaluate whether this advertising model is a good fit for your business.

Be aware that aside from having to heavily discount your product or service, Groupon will take a large chunk out of what money you do collect. So if you own a restaurant and you offer $40 worth of food for $20, Groupon will end up taking around $10, or roughly half, and pass all credit card transaction fees onto you. That means you are, in essence, losing over $30 per Groupon sold. In addition, Groupon customers rarely spend more money above and beyond what the voucher is worth, nor are they likely to return to your establishment in the future without a discount.

So when does Groupon marketing make sense for a business? Here are a few circumstances:

- If your business is brand new, Groupon can bring in that initial wave of customers you need to help get the word out about your existence. In this case, it's okay if you make little to no profit from Groupon users, as you wouldn't be making anything anyway if nobody came in.
- If your business operates on high fixed costs but little to no variable cost per customer - an example of such a business would be one that offers group activities of any type. A dance studio, for instance, would not incur any additional cost if 10 extra students joined an existing class of 20. The 10 new students represent pure profit, so even if they came because of a steep discount, it's worth it.
- If your product or service costs way more than what the Groupon is worth - a LASIK clinic in my neighborhood frequently runs a "$1,000 off of LASIK for $100" deal. In this case they are not offering a very large discount at all, considering that their service typically costs $3,500. They are still netting over $2,500 per Groupon customer for a service with low variable costs.
- If you sell a product or service that requires follow-up purchases - a salon may choose to offer 4 laser hair

removal sessions at a discounted price, knowing that it usually takes 7-8 sessions for the hair to stop growing back altogether. Your hope is that all of these Groupon customers will return to finish the last 3-4 treatments at full price. (However, it's important to note that in reality, because Groupon doesn't restrict deals of the same type from running concurrently, it would be easy for a customer to buy the remaining treatments from a competitor who is offering the same deal. Unfortunately, you won't know the customer return rate until you actually run your deal.)

- If your product or service is so unique that it's unlikely to cross the minds of average consumers - a guided haunted house tour, for example. Most people are not going to be actively searching for something like this, but if they see a deal for it on Groupon while casually browsing, they may think to themselves, "that sounds like fun. I'm in!" So in a way, Groupon promotes impulse purchasing that benefits you as a business.

- If your markup is so high that you can actually make a decent profit after foregoing 75% - there are a lot of offers in the Groupon Goods section that fit into this category. An iPhone accessory that costs $1 to make but retails for $30 will still net you a nice profit of $7.50 (give or take) apiece.

What if none of the above applies to your business? Then the Groupon marketing model is most likely not a good fit for you. But as always, there will be exceptions, so feel free to give it a try.

One solid advantage to utilizing Groupon is that you **will** get customers walking in your door, and fast. Groupon has become so popular that even the most obscure deals have lots of buyers, especially in large metropolitan areas.

So You Sold Some Groupons... Now What?

Once those customers come in, there are a few golden rules you must follow in order to make the most out of your Groupon deal:

- Be prepared to handle the additional workload - while a Groupon salesperson will work with you to decide the max number of vouchers you should sell, only you will truly know how many customers you can comfortably service at a time. Always lean towards the conservative side when estimating your maximum capacity. If your service quality drops because you've brought in more customers than you can handle, you can expect negative reviews to pop up on your local listings shortly, which in the long run will most definitely hurt your business.
- Treat Groupon customers with respect, not contempt - a Groupon customer is not "worth" as much to a business as a customer who's paying full price. Business owners and by extension, their employees, know this and their actions often reflect the bias.

Restaurants, in particular, suffer intensely from this phenomenon. A waiter cringes at the sight of a Groupon because he knows he will be shortchanged on the tip. It doesn't matter that the Groupon mantra is to "always tip on the original value", because in all likelihood, the Groupon customer is going to be a stingy tipper.

You will have to actively train yourself and more importantly, your employees to treat Groupon customers like all your other patrons. You must fight the urge to spend more time with the customer that will yield you the greater profit. Because believe me, Groupon customers will notice, and they tend to be extremely vocal on the Internet.

- Do your best to gather contact information from each Groupon customer - never forget that this customer is not **your** customer just yet! After all, he came in only because he has a Groupon for your establishment. Get him to sign up for your newsletter, like your Facebook page, follow you on Twitter, etc. You need some way to connect with him after he walks out the door. And since you already know that he loves discounts, a coupon for his next visit is a great incentive to offer.
- Get ready to face difficult customers - every once in a while, you've undoubtedly had the displeasure of dealing with a customer who remains unhappy no matter how much you bend over backwards for them. A subset of Groupon customers (roughly 5% according to anecdotal evidence) is the worst of this kind. They will demand to use the Groupon way past its expiration date, attempt to extract even more discounts or freebies out of you, and still complain about everything in the end.

I won't bore you with customer service advice, as I'm sure you've learned how to deal with such customers from past experience. Just be aware that they will come, and be ready for them.

If your first Groupon deal turns a profit, you're probably inclined to run the same offer again, perhaps on another "daily deal" type site. Before you do, consider this: once the word gets out, your repeat customers will come to anticipate your online deals and wait for them. They will rarely, if ever, pay full price again. Your regular prices will become meaningless, and the perceived value of your products or services will drop. As long as you're okay with this, then by all means run more deals. Just remember that past performance isn't necessarily an accurate indicator of the future. Daily deal sites like Groupon are, for the most part, frequently by the same group of people every day. As the novelty of your products or services diminish, so will sales of your voucher.

While your deal is running, be sure to monitor Groupon and other daily deal sites closely. Understand that for many Groupon users, customer loyalty goes out the window as soon as a better deal comes along. You never know when one your competitors will undercut your offer price. While most business owners understand the futility of starting a price war and know that it benefits no one except the end consumer, I've witnessed it on Groupon and similar sites over and over again, especially in the more competitive service industries. Even right now as I write this, there are three very similar Groupon offers for massages available in the Houston area.

One last important point to consider is the fee paid to Groupon for each voucher sold. As stated earlier, 50% is standard. But you should always try to negotiate a more favorable split. Some businesses have been able to reduce the fee down to 40% or less. Even one extra percent can represent considerable dollars in your pocket, depending on the price of your Groupon and how many you sell.

III. Email Marketing

I've mentioned mailing lists quite a few times in earlier chapters, and just like social media, it's simply another way for you to connect with your customers. Email marketing is not nearly as effective as it used to be due to constant spamming. However, if you spend the time to build a relationship with your subscribers, your mailing list can be one of your most valuable assets.

To build a list, you'll need a software program to collect subscriber names and emails for you. My favorite one is Aweber - http://getinternetexposure.com/aweber - it is affordable, starting at only $19 per month, and has all the features you could possibly need. You'll get access to HTML email templates, signup forms, autoresponder support, email open rate and click tracking, plus more.

That means you can easily build stunning forms like these:

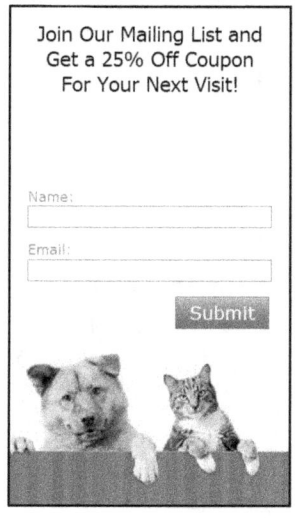
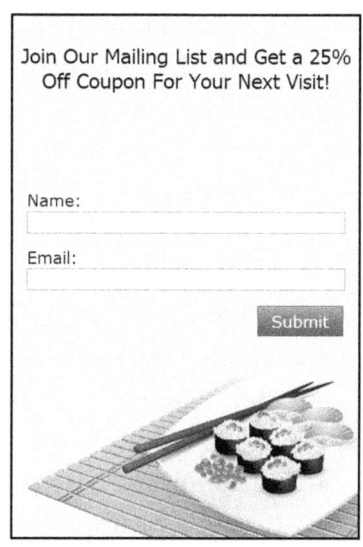

With hundreds of templates to choose from, you'll most definitely find one that fits your website's existing design. It's also very simple to add the signup form you created onto your website. Be sure to place it somewhere conspicuous. It should be in plain view as soon as a visitor lands on your main page.

I suggest that you offer an incentive for signing up, because in this day and age, people are hesitant to give out their email addresses. A discount coupon to your establishment works great, and free information is a popular bribe as well. This can be an e-book or autoresponder series (more on this later), and no matter what industry you're in, you have knowledge that can help people.

So if you're an AC repairman, you can write a short e-book that teaches people how to lower their electricity bills. Offer suggestions like programming their thermostat, changing out their filters often, using more energy-efficient light bulbs, etc. Sure, not all of your tips will have to do with air conditioners directly, but they are still useful related information. Then, at the end of your e-book, you can bring up your company's AC maintenance program and explain to your readers how it can save them even more money on electricity.

Another good thing about using Aweber is that it lets you add an unlimited number of autoresponders. An autoresponder is basically an automated email response sent to each person that signs up for your mailing list. You can set up more than one autoresponder for each list. The first autoresponder will always be dispatched immediately, while any subsequent messages can be scheduled to dispatch x number of days after the previous one.

If you're providing a discount coupon or a free e-book, then all you need is one autoresponder that provides the download link to the coupon or book. But as I alluded to earlier, you can opt to create what's called an autoresponder series instead, if you'd like. Going back to our AC repairman example, you can offer a "7 day e-course on lowering your electricity bills" rather than the e-book. You'll then set your autoresponder sequence up so that when someone signs up for your mailing list, he'll immediately receive lesson 1 via email. He'll receive a new lesson each day thereafter for 6 additional days.

Naturally, you can make the course however long you want. If you have 5 tips total on how to lower electricity bills, then it makes sense to offer a 5 day e-course. Just don't make it too long, because your subscribers will get tired of hearing from you after the 8th or 9th straight day.

The advantage to utilizing an autoresponder series is that the subscriber is reminded of your existence each time he receives a new lesson, whereas an e-book could be forgotten and doomed to collect digital dust as soon as it's downloaded. The downside would be the higher unsubscribe rate, as daily emails can become intrusive even if the subscriber is interested in your information.

Whether you decide to set up autoresponders or not, you'll be able to send out email broadcasts to your subscribers at any time. Do not abuse this privilege, and follow the same rules that apply to social media posts. The majority of your emails should consist mostly of relevant, educational content related to your industry. Advertisements for your products or services can be slipped in casually. Only one out of every five emails should be solely commercial in nature. For these, feel free to advertise your current specials and pitch new products or services. Don't forget to include a strong call to action.

However, unlike social media, you should not blast out frivolous emails that don't contain any useful information, such as one that only wishes everyone a merry Christmas and nothing else. While this kind of post is expected and even welcomed on Facebook, it's simply too trivial as an email broadcast.

When you first start building a list, you may wonder how often you should email your subscribers. Unfortunately, there's no clear answer for that one. Some subscribers are happy to hear from you daily, while others probably can't tolerate your emails more than once a month. In time, as you become more experienced in email marketing, you'll learn the optimal way to go about it. Valuable stats such as your emails' open rates, number of link clicks, number of unsubscribes after each broadcast, and conversion rates for your products or services will all give you immense insight into what works and what doesn't. They're also information you won't be privy to unless you give list building a chance in the first place.

For now, focus on quality over quantity. In other words, as long as your broadcasts are informative and relevant, don't worry about how often you're emailing your subscribers. Understand that you can't please everyone, and some people will unsubscribe no matter how much or how little you email them.

One final tip - with Aweber, you can personalize all your email broadcasts, which I highly suggest that you do. This is why we ask for both the subscriber's name and email address. Instead of a generic salutation like "Dear friend", you can replace "friend" with the subscriber's name. People love seeing their own names written more than any other word. As such, personalizing your emails is one of the best ways to build a rapport with your audience and boost conversion rates.

Personalization is allowed in email subjects as well. Needless to say, a subscriber named John is a lot more likely to open an email with the subject "John, here's your first lesson on lowering your electricity bills" than one without the mention of his name.

It's important to note that some people may input their full name into the signup form, and it would be awkward to use both their first and last names in email broadcasts. Therefore, it's often a better idea to request only their first name on the form.

IV. Tracking Phone Numbers

Most businesses run multiple marketing campaigns simultaneously. If all of those campaigns use the same phone number, then it's impossible to gauge how much return on investment (ROI) each campaign is generating.

This is where tracking phone numbers come in. A tracking phone number is simply a "dummy" number that redirects to a different phone line when dialed and provides a call history for later analysis. It can be extremely valuable if used correctly.

Suppose you're a chiropractor in the Katy area and you're planning to run two different magazine ads. Your phone number will appear on each of these ad copies. You can replace that number with a different tracking phone number on each ad. This way, you'll know exactly how many leads and customers each ad generates.

So let's say that in the past year, your practice has seen anywhere between 10-20 new clients each month. These clients have found you through word of mouth, your website, and local listings. This is the first time you're trying paid advertising. Magazine ad 1 costs $500 and magazine ad 2 costs $1,000. You let the ads run for a month and then evaluate your results. Great news! You've acquired 28 new clients.

If you are not using any tracking phone numbers (i.e. all phone calls go directly to your main office line), you can make the educated guess that the two magazine ads together brought you somewhere between 8-18 new clients last month. You might be right, but you could be

Tracking Phone Numbers

wrong. And you certainly won't know which magazine ad brought in each customer.

By setting up a different tracking phone number for each magazine ad, you can easily gather much more detailed stats. Maybe you learned that magazine 1 has generated 12 phone calls and 3 new clients, while magazine 2 has generated 30 phone calls and 12 new clients. What can you make of this?

You can easily conclude that magazine 2 outperformed magazine 1, even after taking the higher ad cost into consideration. You paid $1,000 for the ad in magazine 2, which means that each phone call cost $33.33 and each new client cost $83.33. As for magazine 1, each phone call cost $41.67 and each new client cost a whopping $166.67! Magazine 2 also yielded a better conversion rate (12 new clients out of 30 phone calls = 40%) than magazine 1 (3 new clients out of 12 phone calls = 25%).

Based on this new information, you can now make smarter marketing decisions. You know the average lifetime value of a customer for your establishment, and with call tracking, you now know how much it's costing you to bring each new customer in the door. You can keep the ad(s) that yield a positive ROI and drop the rest.

Besides magazine ads, you can use tracking phone numbers on many other types of advertisements:

- Marketing videos
- Banner ads
- Postings on Craigslist, Backpage, and other online classifieds
- Newspaper and other print media ads
- Billboards

- Radio and TV ads
- Unconventional advertising (such as sign spinners)

Please be aware that you should never use tracking phone numbers on your website, local listings, or in-house marketing materials (such as business cards, brochures, appointment cards, etc.). You need the information on these important places to stay consistent for the purpose of company branding. Plus, many local listing sites explicitly prohibit the use of tracking phone numbers.

Now let's talk about how to get these tracking numbers set up. There are many web-based call tracking services you can choose from, and many of them are very affordable. Below I've listed some of the best ones:

- http://www.callfire.com - CallFire charges $1/month per phone number, and 5 cents per minute on forwarded calls. CallFire has a very user-friendly interface and a step-by-step setup process.
- http://www.twilio.com - Twilio also charges $1/month per phone number, and they only charge 3 cents per minute on forwarded calls (they advertise 1 cent per minute, but forwarding calls requires the use of their outbound dial API, which is an additional 2 cents per minute). Twilio is not newbie-friendly, and is more geared toward developers than end users. You'll need some understanding of PHP scripting to track calls with it.
- http://www.dynamicic.com - Dynamic Interactive is the most expensive of the three. Their cheapest plan is $49.95 per month for 5 included phone numbers and 750 included minutes. However, their interface is the most user-friendly and they have an excellent customer service team. You can also generate detailed

call reports using many filters, including call length, calls by day of the week, calls by hour of the day, and so on.

For most businesses, CallFire is the best option. Your bill will probably not exceed $10 per month running a few small campaigns at a time. If you expect to run dozens of campaigns simultaneously, it may be worth your while to spend the time or money required to set up Twilio. Choose Dynamic Interactive if you need the advanced reporting options or superior customer support.

By the way, you should always buy local phone numbers, not toll free numbers. Consumers tend to trust local numbers more. Try to get phone numbers that have the same area code as your existing office line. If no such numbers are available, then search for other area codes used by your city or town.

One last topic I want to talk about briefly is SMS (short message service) marketing. Both CallFire and Twilio (but not Dynamic Interactive) support text messaging campaigns. CallFire charges 3 cents per text, while Twilio only charges one cent. The flipside is that CallFire has convenient built-in functions you can use right out of the box, such as the ability to create a subscriber list and send out a text broadcast. For Twilio, you'll need to utilize third-party software or create your own.

SMS marketing works because people are basically glued to their phones all day, every day. Incoming text messages are generally read instantly, or at least as soon as possible. This is a stark contrast to emails, the open rate for which has been declining for over a decade. Today, a typical person's email box is filled with thousands of unread messages. A cell phone with even 5 unread text messages on it would be a rare find.

However, SMS marketing is not suitable for all industries. It is a lot more personal than what most consumers are used to, and you must tread carefully. If you offer a product or service that the average person rarely needs, then limit your texts to appointment reminders and *maybe* one special offer every few months. For example, people don't want to hear from an AC repairman unless their AC isn't working, especially not in the form of a text message on their personal phones. In this case, if the AC company decides to send out a text broadcast, they'd better offer something very enticing that's not contingent on broken AC units (such as a free or discounted AC performance checkup).

Restaurants seem to benefit from SMS marketing the most. After all, everybody has to eat. Send out enticing offers an hour or two before the usual mealtimes and you'll be loved. I know that personally, when 5 o' clock rolls around, I start thinking about dinner plans. A well timed text from my local diner always catches my attention, and I do go there quite a bit.

But even if you do own a restaurant, never, **ever** spam your SMS subscriber list. Text spam is not a problem in the United States yet, but in some Asian countries, especially China, it's rampant. The result? People basically ignore any text message that's not from someone on their contact list. This is what happens when advertisers abuse their subscriber list. So heed my warning and send out one offer per week, max. I'd suggest that once every two weeks or less is more ideal. Monitor your list closely, and if a lot of people are unsubscribing, then you're probably texting them too often.

Also, do not, under any circumstances, broadcast to people who didn't opt-in to your list. Just because they gave you their phone number when they ordered your product or service doesn't mean they want to receive texts from you. Doing so will not only breed ill will with those customers, but also possibly land you in some hot water with the law. Just don't do it.

In addition, you should provide an easy way for people to unsubscribe from your list. The standard approach is for them to reply "STOP" to a text message. Include these instructions after every text broadcast you send. Make sure that the software you are using actually does honor such requests. If a customer texts "STOP" and continues to receive your texts, you're asking for trouble even if the software failure is not technically your fault.

V. Outsourcing

As a local business owner, every Internet related task can and should be outsourced if you have the budget for it. I'm sure you as an entrepreneur understand the value of time. You probably started your business in the first place because you wanted the freedom associated with being your own boss. But you soon found out that running a business requires skills far beyond the actual services you provide to customers. You now have to deal with accounting, people management, customer service, marketing, and more. Your choices are to do them yourself, hire employees, or outsource.

Of course, we both know that it's impossible to do everything yourself, unless you want to be a slave to your business. Plus, those tasks are most likely not part of your skill set. Internet marketing in particular is one of those constantly changing fields with an extremely steep learning curve. It's a field that if you truly wish to become effective at, you have to devote a huge amount of time into; time you probably don't have and most certainly don't want to waste.

How much is your time worth? If you make $100,000 per year working 40 hours per week, your time is worth $50 per hour, give or take. That means if you can get someone else to do your Internet marketing work for less than that, it's a no-brainer. This is especially true if they can do the work faster and better than you can, which will likely be the case since that's what they do for a living.

To put it another way, suppose that you're a successful chiropractor and you've been in business for 20 years. Back in the 1990's and early 2000's, Yellow Pages was still the name of the game and you didn't need to advertise on the Internet. You used the Internet to exchange emails with out-of-town family members and that's about it. Then one day you realized that you weren't getting as many new customers as before. You research for a bit and find out that people are now looking for chiropractors on the Internet, not on the Yellow Pages. But you have no idea how to find customers online. Heck, you don't even know how to get a website.

You may feel like that this change in the way consumers find businesses happened suddenly. But in fact, it was a very gradual process. It's just that you, like most local business owners, didn't notice until the transformation started to negatively affect your income.

Then, you probably decided to learn how Internet marketing works. You try a few things here and there, maybe put up a basic website with the help of a hosting company's template. You create a Facebook fan page, easy enough. Perhaps you tried Google Adwords and lost some money, and subsequently decided that it didn't work.

But let me ask you: if your air conditioner broke down, would you try to fix it yourself? Most of you wouldn't. If you're seriously ill, would you try to diagnose and treat yourself? For your sake, I hope not.

So why would you attempt to do your own marketing, which is arguably the most important facet of your business, if you have no prior experience and zero idea on how to properly go about it?

I would wager that marketing your local business on the Internet is more important than you currently think it is, and will only become more so as time goes on. If you approach it yourself halfheartedly, you won't even scratch your competitors who have professional teams putting 110% effort into it.

You may be wondering, what's the point of the rest of this book if I'm just going to recommend that you outsource everything? The answer is simple - you need a good understanding of Internet marketing so you can avoid being scammed. Everyone and their brother can claim to be an "Internet guru", "Internet marketer", or "local consultant", among other similar titles. You probably get calls and letters from such individuals every single day. Most of them have no idea what they're talking about and certainly do not know what they're doing when it comes to Internet marketing. They could have read a few articles on Search Engine Land and suddenly, armed with that tiny bit of knowledge, act like they know everything. And they can easily win you over because they do in fact know more than you, even if it's just by a little.

With what you learned from this book, you can now interview these so-called Internet marketing experts to determine their true level of expertise. You're much more likely to find a company who can back up what they promise and generate more leads for your business from the Internet than you thought were possible.

Also, now that you're armed with knowledge, you certainly have the option of tackling any of these tasks yourself. Maybe you just don't have the budget to outsource right now, or you're interested in a certain promotional method and want to play around with it. Either way, you'd no longer have to run in there totally lost.

In any case, if you've decided to outsource, you can choose to either hire a local firm or one from overseas. There are advantages and disadvantages to both,

Outsourcing

but I always recommend that you hire someone local. A local Internet marketer knows your city's style, atmosphere, and people. They understand how to appeal to their target audience and is able to create credible, convincing content. Since they live nearby, you can choose to meet them in person before deciding whether or not they are a good fit.

The only positive aspect to outsourcing overseas is the lower cost. You'll continuously run into snags due to the language barrier, especially since you're often corresponding about your specific profession, which a non-native English speaker isn't likely to know the lingo of. Content created by overseas firms may be riddled with spelling and grammar errors as well as improper syntax. Neither search engines nor human readers will appreciate such low quality content. In addition, you'll obviously be located in different time zones and communication can be a problem.

Hiring locally will cost you considerably more, and you may find that even prices from marketing firms in your immediate area can differ drastically. But price should never be your sole determining factor for hiring someone. In this industry, you get what you pay for. Instead, you should be far more focused on how well they can pass your proficiency test.

Be wary of companies who offer flat rate services. Each business has different needs, and a marketing method that performs spectacularly in one industry could completely flop in another. A good company will always provide you with a custom quote, taking into account what strategies you already have in place and what areas need improvement. Companies that embrace the "one size fits all" philosophy will not take the time to get to know your business, your goals, and your unique requirements, resulting in less effective campaigns.

Once you've chosen a company to work with, don't go overboard with the haggling. Remember, a truly capable Internet marketing company is not desperate for more clients, and will not negotiate pricing with you. They know their services will result in a positive return on investment (ROI) for you, and they'll charge accordingly.

9. Conclusion

Internet exposure is fundamental to the very survival of your local business. You really only have two options here - either ignore the Internet and bite the dust, or incorporate all that it has to offer and crush your competition. We hope we've convinced you to choose the latter.

Be sure to sign up for our free newsletter at http://getinternetexposure.com. Remember, Internet marketing is an ever-changing field, and what's working today may no longer work tomorrow. It pays to stay updated.

If, like most local business owners, you want to take the next step but just don't have the time, we can help. Our company specializes in local marketing and we have helped hundreds of clients achieve a level of income they never thought was possible, all thanks to the Internet. We only work with one business per industry in each city, and we'll absolutely commit ourselves to their total Internet domination.

If you're interested, please visit our new client page below for more information:

http://getinternetexposure.com/newclient

As a final word, we want to congratulate you on making it this far. You now know more about Internet marketing than 99% of all local business owners out there. Whether you decide to embark on this journey yourself or hire someone else, you are now ready to take that first step.

Either way, take our advice and start today. Don't wait until tomorrow, because "tomorrow" may never come. The sooner you take action, the sooner you'll start seeing results.

Once again, thank you for reading, and we wish you the very best.

- Sherry and Daisy

www.ingramcontent.com/pod-product-compliance
Lightning Source LLC
Chambersburg PA
CBHW061512180526
45171CB00001B/146